ADVANCE PRAISE

'This valuable book brings much-needed clarity to the contentious debate about the history of Easter. Scholarly, cogent and informative, it provides a thorough and authoritative analysis of the competing arguments and myths. Richard Sermon not only skillfully explores the medieval evidence, but also shows how modern misconceptions about this subject have developed and spread. This is essential reading for anyone interested in Anglo-Saxon paganism and the history of the festival year.'

> **– Eleanor Parker**
> Author of *Winters in the World: A Journey through the Anglo-Saxon Year*

'A well-documented, multi-disciplinary journey through space and time, *Easter: A Pagan Goddess, a Christian Holiday and their Contested History* has to be essential reading for anyone interested in either the pagan religions of England or the background of the word Easter. Chasing down the bunnies and delving deep inside the dark spaces that lurk inside the chocolate eggs, this wide-ranging and carefully researched book undertakes a worthy Arthurian quest to trace the pre-Christian background of our modern-day Easter festival and the traditions associated with it.'

> **– Terry Gunnell**
> Professor Emeritus of Folkloristics, University of Iceland

EASTER

A PAGAN GODDESS, A CHRISTIAN HOLIDAY, AND
THEIR CONTESTED HISTORY

EASTER

A PAGAN GODDESS, A CHRISTIAN HOLIDAY, AND THEIR CONTESTED HISTORY

BY

RICHARD SERMON

UPPSALA BOOKS

London

UPPSALA BOOKS

London

www.uppsalabooks.com

Copyright © Uppsala Books 2024

ISBN 978-1-961361-16-4 Hardback

ISBN 978-1-961361-17-1 Paperback

CONTENTS

FIGURES

Figure 1. Diagrammatic reconstruction of the Anglo-Saxon year based on surviving Old English sources (drawn by the author).

Figure 2. Late fourth-century BC terracotta dish from Apuia in Italy depicting the arrival of Eos in her horse drawn chariot.

Figure 3. Arminius Monument (Hermannsdenkmal) constructed in the Teutoburg forest near Detmold in 1875.

Figure 4. Carl Emil Doepler's (1824–1905) depiction of the Norse goddess 'Frigg as Ostara' first published in 1882.

Figure 5. Johannes Gehrts' (1855–1921) depiction of a radiant Ostara above her Germanic followers, published in 1885.

Figure 6. Cover of Ostara magazine (reprint of first issue) published in Vienna by Jörg Lanz von Liebenfels in 1930.

Figure 7. Osterräder (Easter-wheel) with Ostara motto and Osterdechen song (1929/1930) on a locally printed postcard (reproduced courtesy of Andreas Marz, Osterdechen, Lügde).

Figure 8. Diagrammatic representation of the Wiccan 'Wheel of the Year' (drawn by the author).

Figure 9. Map of north-west Europe showing the principal locations discussed in the final chapters, with inset example of the Morken-Harff altar stones (drawn by the author).

Figure 10. Plan of Yeavering's structure E, showing the free-standing post and nine arcs of the timber foundations in grey, and three sunrise alignments in black (drawn by the author).

ACKNOWLEDGEMENTS

I am grateful to: Dr Malcolm Jones (former Senior Lecturer in the Department of English Language and Linguistics at the University of Sheffield and Assistant Director of the National Centre for English Cultural Tradition) for his support and encouragement of my initial articles on Anglo-Saxon calendrics (Sermon 2002 and 2008); Dr Jessica Hemming and Dr Antone Minard (Editor and Assistant Editor of *Folklore*), and their expert referee Dr Patrizia de Bernardo Stempel, for their constructive comments and helpful advice in relation to my more recent article on *Eostre* (Sermon 2022); Dr Caroline Oates (Librarian and Administrator for the Folklore Society) and Emma Lockwood (Portfolio Manager at Taylor & Francis) for their approval to incorporate and expand this article into the current book; and to the co-founders of Uppsala Books, Dr Tom Shippey (former teacher of Old English at six universities, including Oxford and Harvard) and Professor Leonard Neidorf (an authority on *Beowulf* and Professor of English at Nanjing University), for suggesting the book title and kindly inviting me to submit this contribution to their series.

INTRODUCTION

At the time of writing this book I look back to find that I have been somewhat preoccupied with the subject of the Easter for more than thirty years—including its history, traditions and folk-lore, but most of all the origins of its unusual name in the English language. For me this all began on Easter Monday in 1993 when I was visiting my parents at our family home 'in the flat, wheat-growing north-east corner of Oxfordshire' (Thompson 1957, 1). Brown hares were a common sight at that time of year in the fields and pasture that surrounded the village, as described by the local author Flora Thompson:

> Just as the last group was nearing the stile and the children were breathing a sigh of relief at not having been seen and scolded, a hare broke from one of the hedges and went bounding and ca-pering across the field in the headlong way hares have. It looked for a moment as if it would land under the feet of the last group of men, who were nearing the stile; but, suddenly, it scented danger and drew up and squatted motionless behind a tuft of green clover a few feet from the pathway. (Thompson 1957, 162)

It was in this environment that I sat down to watch the BBC's *Wildlife on One* Easter Special entitled 'Shadow of the Hare' (Nicholls 1993). The television programme was narrated by Sir David Attenborough and included a specially commissioned folk song 'The Fabled Hare' written and performed by Maddy Prior

1

(1993). As might be expected from a BBC wildlife documentary, the description of the brown hare's (*Lepus europaeus*) life cycle and natural history, along with the high-quality filming, were both informative and captivating. However, for me, the most intriguing elements of the programme were its surprising claims regarding the folklore of the hare, and its alleged role (along with Easter eggs) as an ancient symbol of the Anglo-Saxon goddess *Eostre*, as described in the following extract from David Attenborough's narration:

> In its original guise the hare was not a witch, but the symbol of an ancient Saxon goddess... Spring was the time of Eastre [*sic*] the Anglo-Saxon goddess of fertility and rebirth, and her sacred beast was the hare. The hare carried the new light that warmed the crops and brought to the fields Eastre's ultimate symbol of fertility, the egg... A symbol of spring and the reawakening year... Parts of Britain's pagan beliefs were thinly disguised and absorbed into the new religion. Eastre's festival of the rebirth of the year became a festival celebrating the rebirth of Christ, and Easter still carries her name. Eastre's eggs, her symbols of fertility also survive, though now they are made of chocolate. But the hare was too vivid a pagan symbol to become part of a Christian festival, instead it was disguised as rabbit and dressed up to look ridiculous. It became the Easter bunny.

And repeated in a more lyrical fashion by Maddy Prior (1993, verses 3–4):

> I am companion to the Gods,
> I can conceive while I am pregnant;
> I call the dawn and spring in,
> I am the advent.
>
> I bring life from water,
> In a cup that must be broken;
> I whisper to the bursting egg,

I'm Aestre's [*sic*] token.

An accompanying article by Gareth Davies (1993) in the *Radio Times* magazine reiterated these claims that: (a) *Eostre* was the Anglo-Saxon goddess of spring and the dawn, (b) who was symbolised by the hare and the egg as 'the ultimate symbol of fertility and rebirth', and (c) whose name, festival and symbols were appropriated by later Christians for the festival celebrating Jesus' resurrection.

I had briefly heard of *Eostre* during my undergraduate studies in a lecture on Anglo-Saxon religion and burial practice, but it was this documentary that prompted my long-standing interest in *Eostre* and Bede's description of the pagan Anglo-Saxon year. Since that time, and with the rapid growth of the internet, these claims are repeated every Easter with Google search results for 'Eostre' and 'Ostara' now totalling almost 7.9 million in April 2024. The purpose of this book is to explore the principal claims and counterclaims that now surround the goddess *Eostre* and the origins of the Christian paschal (Easter) festival by critically examining the substance and genealogy of these ideas and theories from their earliest sources to the present day. The book incorporates and expands upon ideas outlined in previous articles (Sermon 2002 and 2008), notably in an article published in the journal *Folklore* focussing on the relationship between the goddess *Eostre* and the Gallo-Roman or Romano-Germanic cult of the *Matronae Austriahenae* (Sermon 2022).

We will begin by exploring the origins of the Christian festival (Latin *Pascha*) with its roots in the Jewish Passover and Hebrew lunar calendar, and how this festival became established in late Roman Britain with three British bishops attending the Council of Arles in 314 AD where the date of the festival was discussed. While the native British and Irish referred to their Christian festival as *Pasc* (Old Welsh) and *Cásc* (Old Irish), the Anglo-Saxon migration and settlement of lowland Britain (in what was to become

England) saw the arrival of a Germanic form of paganism and the initial retreat of Christianity. However, by the end of the seventh century the Anglo-Saxon kingdoms had all officially converted to Christianity, and yet their name for the Paschal festival *Eastron* (Old English) had, according to the Venerable Bede (672–735 AD), derived from the name of a pagan goddess *Eostre*. We then go on to consider a possible parallel in Germany with the Paschal festival name *Ostern* (*Ostarun* in Old High German), and whether this provides evidence of a common Proto-Germanic goddess with origins perhaps going back to an even earlier Indo-European dawn goddess. The Paschal festival's symbols (primarily eggs, rabbits and hares), its English and German vernacular names and its timing have all been claimed and disputed by various German nationalist, occultist, neopagan and modern Wiccan groups—examples of which are explored in more detail. Finally, we will examine the possible relationship between *Eostre* and a group of Roman altars from Lower Rhine region dedicated to the *Matronae Austriahenae*, and look at a unique wedge-shaped structure revealed during excavations at the seventh-century royal site of Yeavering in Northumberland, which may provide the first evidence in support of Bede's Anglo-Saxon calendar.

In these chapters I demonstrate the fallacy of neopagan claims that the early Christians (living around the eastern Mediterranean) appropriated either the name, timing or symbols of their Paschal festival from a yet to be recorded Anglo-Saxon (or Germanic) goddess. Nevertheless, I also argue that it seems doubtful that Bede, as a devout Christian scholar and historian, would have fabricated a pagan goddess (and her month) in order to explain the Old English vernacular name for the Paschal festival. On balance, I suggest that the German festival name *Ostern* is more likely to be a loan word from Old English resulting from Anglo-Saxon missionary activity in Germany during the eighth century, although this does not preclude the existence of an ancestral Proto-Germanic goddess cult or a possible relationship to an earlier Indo-European dawn goddess. With regard to the various folk customs, symbols, place names and locations that are often said to have been associated with the goddess *Eostre*, and/or her reconstructed German equivalent *Ostara*, none of these claims stand up to close scrutiny. The Wiccan neopagan calendar or 'Wheel of the Year' is known to be a composite construction first outlined by the religion's founder in 1954, with the festival name *Ostara* (for the spring equinox) added by an American follower in 1974. More recently it has been suggested (Shaw 2011) that *Eostre* was a 'local group-specific goddess' at Eastry in Kent and compared to the cult of the *Matronae Austriahenae* in north-west Germany. However, there is no clear evidence to support such a comparison, which ignores the one piece of evidence Bede provides about her cult, specifically the timing of her month and celebrations. In the end we are left with just Bede's account of the goddess *Eostre* and his description of the pagan Anglo-Saxon year; nevertheless, in the final chapter I build on initial observations made by Richard North (2012) to offer a revised interpretation Yeavering's enigmatic 'theatre' structure.

Old English Pronunciation

In Old English of the Anglo-Saxon period the letters *þ* (thorn) and *ð* (eth) represent the two sounds which are now written *th*, the letters *sc* represent the sound which is now written *sh*, and in the word *Geola* (Yule), the letter *g* represents the sound which is now written *y*.

CHAPTER 1

Pesach to *Pascha*:

The Jewish Origins of a Christian Festival

In order to unravel the web of confusion and misinformation that often surrounds the origins of the Easter festival, we first need to understand that for the majority of the world it does not bear the name 'Easter' or anything like it. In the English-speaking world this confusion is compounded by a general decline in Christian knowledge among the wider population, with a corresponding rise in secularism and alternative spirituality. The present chapter will therefore attempt to fill this gap by assuming no prior knowledge of the biblical narrative or Jewish and early Christian history.

Thus we begin with the story the prophet Moses and the Israelites' captivity and enslavement in Egypt, as described in the book of Exodus (1–6). Whilst there is no archaeological or hieroglyphic evidence to support the biblical account, it forms one of the foundation myths of the Jewish people. In order to free his people from captivity Moses warns Pharaoh of ten plagues that God then visits upon Egyptians (Exodus 7–12). Before the final plague the Israelites are told to sacrifice and feast upon an unblemished lamb, and to daub the blood of the lamb on the door posts of their houses. These acts are carried out so that God would recognise, and 'pass over' (Hebrew *pasach* פָּסַח), the homes of the Israelites while taking the lives of the first-born sons of the Egyptians:

> And thus shall ye eat it; with your loins girded, your shoes on
> your feet, and your staff in your hand; and ye shall eat it in haste:
> it is the Lord's passover. For I will pass through the land of Egypt
> this night, and will smite all the firstborn in the land of Egypt,
> both man and beast; and against all the gods of Egypt I will ex-
> ecute judgment: I am the Lord. And the blood shall be to you
> for a token upon the houses where ye are: and when I see the
> blood, I will pass over you, and the plague shall not be upon you
> to destroy you, when I smite the land of Egypt. (*King James Bible*,
> Exodus 12:11–13)

Following this plague, the Israelites are said to have made their
escape from Egypt across the Red Sea and into the Sinai desert.
However, with little time to prepare they could take only unleavened bread on their long journey, which many years later at the
end of Moses' life brought them to the 'promised land' of Canaan
(Deuteronomy 34). The Israelites (including the later Jews and Samaritans) were commanded to remember these events each year
at the Passover (Hebrew *Pesach* פֶּסַח) festival. Over these seven
days, which begin with the evening *Seder* meal of lamb, wine and
other symbolic foods, only unleavened bread or *matzah* is permit-
ted.

The Bible later records that following the death of Israelite
King Solomon, perhaps around 931 BC, his people and territory
were divided between the northern Kingdom of Israel centred on
Samaria and the southern Kingdom of Judah centred on Jerusalem
(I Kings 11–12). Both kingdoms were to come under increasing
pressure from Aramaic-speaking powers to the north-east in what
is now Syria, Iraq and western Iran. The first of these great powers
was the Assyrian Empire, which conquered the Kingdom of Israel
in around 720 BC (II Kings 17), and was succeeded by Babylonian
Empire, which finally conquered the Kingdom of Judah in around
587 BC (II Kings 24–25). With their temple in Jerusalem de-

stroyed the people of Judah (the Jews) were not only subdued, but many were then exiled to Babylon on the banks of rivers Tigris and Euphrates:

> By the rivers of Babylon, there we sat down,
>
> Yea, we wept, when we remembered Zion...
>
> How shall we sing the Lord's song in a strange land?
>
> (*King James Bible*, Psalm 137:1 and 4)

This exile was to have a number of significant impacts on the development of Jewish identity and culture, two of which are particularly relevant to our discussion here. The first of these impacts was linguistic with the loss of Hebrew as a spoken language among the Jews (and Samaritans) and its replacement by Aramaic as the common language of the region. With this came a need for Aramaic translations (*Targum*) and interpretations (*Talmud*) of the Hebrew law (*Torah*) and wider biblical texts (*Tanach*). Thus, the Hebrew festival name *Pesach* became *Pascha* (פַּסְחָא) in Aramaic. Their obvious similarity is due to both names deriving from the same North Semitic root meaning to 'skip', 'omit' or 'pass over' with cognates already existing in both languages. The second of these impacts was calendric with the Jews adopting of the Babylonian lunisolar calendar, which is based on a 'common' lunar year (354 days) comprised of twelve alternate 29 and 30-day lunar months, with an additional intercalary month added every second or third 'embolismic' year to correct the accumulated annual shortfall (11 days) with a normal solar year (365 days). Each month begins at the new moon with the full moon appearing roughly halfway through the month, usually on days 14 to 15 (see table 1).

Month	Hebrew Name	Common Year Days	Embolismic Year Days	Approximation
1	*Nisan*	30	30	March / April
2	*Iyar*	29	29	April / May
3	*Sivan*	30	30	May / June
4	*Tamuz*	29	29	June / July
5	*Av*	30	30	July / August
6	*Elul*	29	29	August / September
7	*Tishri*	30	30	September / October
8	*Cheshvan*	29 (+1 complete years)	29 (+1 complete years)	October / November
9	*Kislev*	30 (−1 deficient years)	30 (−1 deficient years)	November / December
10	*Tevet*	29	29	December / January
11	*Shvat*	30	30	January / February
12	*Adar I*	29	30	February / March
13	*Adar II*	0	29	(Intercalary month)
Year Subtypes		**Common Year Totals**	**Embolismic Year Totals**	
Deficient		353	383	
Regular		354	384	
Complete		355	385	

Table 1. Months of the Hebrew–Babylonian lunisolar calendar (Sadinoff 1992; Walker 2015).

According to the biblical commandments the Passover was to be celebrated in the first month of the year (Exodus 12:2), with the sacrificial offering and *Seder* meal taking place on the evening of the fourteenth day (Exodus 12:6-8) and continuing over the next seven days with the Feast of Unleavened Bread until the evening of the twenty-first day (Exodus 12:18). Before their exile this had been during the Israelite and formerly Canaanite month of *Aviv* meaning 'spring' (Exodus 13:4, 23:15, 34:18; Deuteronomy 16:1), but with the adoption of the Babylonian calendar it became the month of *Nisan* (Esther 3:7); with the intention that Passover should begin on the first full moon on or after the spring (vernal) equinox. It is for this reason that the date of the Passover festival moves each year relative to the Roman (Julian and later Gregorian) solar calendar (see table 2).

Hebrew Date	Lunar Year	Week Day	Julian Date	Solar Year	Full Moon
14 Nisan 3784	Embolismic complete	Wednesday	12 April 24 AD	Leap	0
14 Nisan 3785	Common complete	Monday	2 April 25AD	Normal	−1
14 Nisan 3786	Common regular	Friday	22 March 26 AD	Normal	0
14 Nisan 3787	Embolismic deficient	Wednesday	9 April 27 AD	Normal	0
14 Nisan 3788	Common complete	Monday	29 March 28 AD	Leap	0
14 Nisan 3789	Embolismic deficient	Saturday	16 April 29 AD	Normal	+1
14 Nisan 3790	Common regular	Wednesday	5 April 30 AD	Normal	+1
14 Nisan 3791	Common complete	Monday	26 March 31 AD	Normal	+1
14 Nisan 3792	Embolismic complete	Monday	14 April 32 AD	Leap	0
14 Nisan 3793	Common regular	Friday	3 April 33AD	Normal	0
14 Nisan 3794	Common deficient	Monday	22 March 34AD	Normal	+1
14 Nisan 3795	Embolismic complete	Monday	11 April 35 AD	Normal	0
14 Nisan 3796	Common regular	Friday	30 March 36 AD	Leap	0
14 Nisan 3797	Common complete	Wednesday	20 March 37 AD	Normal	0
14 Nisan 3798	Embolismic deficient	Monday	7 April 38 AD	Normal	+1
14 Nisan 3799	Common regular	Friday	27 March 39 AD	Normal	+1
14 Nisan 3800	Embolismic complete	Friday	15 April 40 AD	Leap	0
14 Nisan 3801	Common deficient	Monday	3 April 41 AD	Normal	+2
14 Nisan 3802	Common complete	Saturday	24 March 42 AD	Normal	+1
14 Nisan 3803	Embolismic regular	Friday	12 April 43 AD	Normal	+1

Table 2. Julian dates for the Eve of Passover (24–43 AD) according to Rabbinic reckoning, and astronomical full moons ± 1 day (Sadinoff 1992; Walker 1997 and 2015).

Following the fall of Babylon to the Persians in 539 BC the Jews were allowed to return to Judea and to rebuild their holy temple in Jerusalem. During this period of the Second Temple (c. 516 BC to 70 AD) the Jews would take their sacrificial offerings (a lamb or kid-goat) to the temple priests at Passover—a practice which the Samaritans still maintain at their ancient temple site on Mount Gerizim. However, by the first century AD, having previously thrown off the rule of the Greeks, Judea was once again dominated by a foreign empire, but this time it was that of Rome. As the Jews became angered by the brutality of Roman rule and interference in their religious affairs there was a growing restlessness among the population. This was linked to a longing for the Messiah promised by the prophets—an anointed king of the Jews who would unite his people and liberate them from the rule of Rome and its Herodian client kings.

It is in this context that we need to understand the life of Jesus, a Jew from the town of Nazareth in Galilee, and his teachings on the spiritual, rather than physical, liberation of his people. However, this is a difference that was almost certainly lost on his Roman executioners, who would simply have viewed him and his followers as a threat to public order and Roman rule over Judea. Jesus was said to have been crucified either on (John 19:14) or after (Matthew 26:19; Mark 14:16; Luke 22:13) the eve of Passover, with the 3 April 33 AD and 7 April 30 AD being the most favoured dates respectively. The Last Supper was almost certainly a Jewish *Seder* meal, with its symbolic use of the unleavened bread and wine; and his crucifixion on a Friday, which was the eve of the Jewish sabbath, necessitated his hastened death and burial before sunset. Three days later, on the Sunday, his body was claimed to have been missing from the tomb, leading to one of the central beliefs in Christian theology: Jesus' bodily resurrection and subsequent ascension to Heaven.

The Gospel accounts of Jesus' life and teachings were written in Koine Greek, which was the common language of the eastern Roman and later Byzantine empires. Many Jews had already settled in the Greek-speaking cities and ports of the eastern Mediterranean, including Alexandria where a Greek translation of the Hebrew 'Old Testament' had been completed by the late second century BC. This translation, known as the *Septuagint*, simply transliterated the Aramaic Passover name *Pascha* (פַּסְחָא) into Greek characters (Πάσχα). Furthermore, it was within these Graeco-Jewish communities that early Christianity (initially seen as a Jewish sect) began to take hold and was adopted by their gentile neighbours. It is therefore not surprising that the Greek 'New Testament' and liturgy should use *Pascha* as the name for both the Jewish Passover and the Christian Feast of the Resurrection—a shared meaning still expressed by the English (via Latin and Old French) adjective 'paschal'.

From the first century AD these early Christians were subjected to sporadic periods of intense persecution, often due to their rejection of the religious cult and deification of the Roman emperor. However, their position was to be completely transformed with the conversion to Christianity of the Emperor Constantine (the Great) in 312 AD. The following year saw the issuing of the Edict of Milan, which granted official toleration to the Christian religion, and from this point in Constantine's reign (306–337 AD) Christianity began to emerge as the dominant religion of the Roman Empire. Nevertheless, the forms of Christian doctrine and worship varied greatly across the empire, and in order to standardise them Constantine convened the Council of Nicaea in 325 AD. This meeting of bishops resulted in the Nicene Creed (a single Christian doctrine), which is still followed by most Orthodox, Catholic and Protestant churches today, and rulings on the observance of the Feast of the Resurrection.

The early Christians are known to have celebrated their Paschal festival in accordance with the timing of the Jewish Passover. However, adhering to the Hebrew calendar meant that the day commemorating Jesus' resurrection would not always fall on a Sunday, and would often occur on other days of the week. Following the Council of Nicaea, it was ruled that the Paschal festival should be observed on 'the first Sunday after the full moon, on or after the vernal equinox'. The ecclesiastical vernal equinox was fixed as the 21st of March, which means that Easter must be celebrated on a Sunday between the 22nd of March and the 25th of April. The Paschal full moon is calculated using a nineteen-year cycle first established by the church in Alexandria, and then developed in the sixth century by Dionysius Exiguus, but does not always coincide with the astronomical full moon. Evidence of this method can be seen in the Ravenna Paschal Calendar, a marble slab displayed in the Museum of Ravenna Cathedral in northern Italy, which uses concentric circles to illustrate the five nineteen-year cycles of the Paschal full moon (and following Resurrection

Sunday dates) from 532 to 626 AD (Detoma 2018).

With the translation of the Greek bible into Vulgate (common) Latin by St Jerome in the late fourth century, *Pascha* became the universal name for the Christian Feast of the Resurrection in both the Greek-speaking eastern (later Byzantine) empire centred on Constantinople, and the Latin-speaking western empire centred on Rome. The name then passed into the vernacular Latin languages of western Europe and survives in all their modern descendants: including Italian *Pasqua*, French *Pâques*, Spanish *Pascua*, Portuguese *Páscoa* and Romanian *Paşti*. Nevertheless, the date on which the Paschal festival is now celebrated reveals a continuing divide between the ancient branches of eastern and western Christendom. Both Christian traditions use the same formula (quoted above) for calculating the date of the Paschal festival, and for most of their history celebrated the Feast of the Resurrection on the same day and date, until the late sixteenth century. This agreement was based on their shared use of Julian calendar, which was introduced by the Emperor Julius Caesar in 46–45 BC and is virtually identical to our modern western (Gregorian) calendar, apart from the rules concerning the designation of normal (365 day) and leap (366 day) years. The Julian solar year is reckoned to be 365.25 days long, which can be accommodated by one simple calendric rule where 'every year that is exactly divisible by four is a leap year'. However, the length of the solar year is in fact closer to 365.2422 days, and thus the Julian calendar gains about 0.78 days per century relative to the astronomical solstices and equinoxes. This cumulative error continued to increase until 1582 when the Gregorian calendar reform was introduced in by Pope Gregory XIII. This reform included an exception to the Julian leap year rule (above) 'for years exactly divisible by 100 and not by 400' resulting in a much closer average year of 365.2425 days. Notwithstanding the logic behind this reform, the eastern Orthodox church continues to use Julian calendar, which is currently running thirteen days behind the Gregorian calendar used in the western Catholic and Protestant churches.

Year AD	Eve of Passover (*Erev Pesach*)	Difference (days)	Paschal Full Moon (Ecclesiastical)	Resurrection Sunday (Easter Sunday)
2004	5 April	0	5 April	11 April
2005	23 April	−29	25 March	27 March
2006	12 April	+1	13 April	16 April
2007	2 April	0	2 April	8 April
2008	19 April	−28	22 March	23 March
2009	8 April	+2	10 April	12 April
2010	29 March	+1	30 March	4 April
2011	18 April	−1	17 April	24 April
2012	6 April	+1	7 April	8 April
2013	25 March	+2	27 March	31 March
2014	14 April	0	14 April	20 April
2015	3 April	0	3 April	5 April
2016	22 April	−30	23 March	27 March
2017	10 April	+1	11 April	16 April
2018	30 March	+1	31 March	1 April
2019	19 April	−1	18 April	21 April
2020	8 April	0	8 April	12 April
2021	27 March	+1	28 March	4 April
2022	15 April	+1	16 April	17 April
2023	5 April	0	5 April	9 April

Table 3. Gregorian dates for the Jewish Eve of Passover, Christian Paschal Full Moon and Resurrection Sunday over a nineteen-year lunar cycle (2004–2023 AD).

In summary, the Feast of the Resurrection (or Paschal festival) is a Christian holiday that was neither assimilated or 'stolen' from the pagans—whether ancient, modern, or anywhere in between. If anything, the holiday was borrowed from Jewish tradition and celebrates the most central events in the life of Jesus: with the Last Supper almost certainly being a Passover *Seder* meal, his crucifixion taking place on a Friday that was either the eve or during Passover, and his claimed resurrection three days later, on a Sunday. The annual festival commemorating these events derives its Latin name *Pascha* (via Greek and Aramaic) from the Hebrew name for the Jewish Passover (*Pesach*), which celebrates the Bible story of Moses, and the Israelites escape from captivity in Egypt, where God took the lives of the first-born sons of the Egyptians, but spared or 'passed over' those of the Israelites. It is under this name, or a version of it, that most of the (non-English-speaking) world knows the Christian festival. The timing of this 'moveable feast' is again rooted in Jewish tradition and the Hebrew lunisolar calendar. While the Early Christians are known to have followed Jewish practice in fixing the date of the Paschal festival, after the Council of Nicaea in 325 AD the current formula for calculating the festival date was established, ensuring it always fell on a Sunday. Nevertheless, the calendric relationship between the Jewish and Christian festivals is still apparent today (see table 3). Therefore, it is spurious to suggest that the Early Church (centred around the eastern Mediterranean) would have named and timed its most important festival after that of a (yet to be recorded) north European pagan goddess.

CHAPTER 2

Pascha to *Pasg*:

The Paschal Festival in Roman and Post-Roman Britain

The island of Britain was known to the geographers of the ancient world, who were aware of its wealth in natural resources and rich agricultural land. During Julius Caesar's military campaigns and conquests in Gaul he made two expeditions to Britain in 55 and 54 BC, and although he subdued the local tribes he encountered, he did not leave any permanent Roman settlement or garrison on the island. It was not until 43 AD that the Roman Emperor Claudius ordered the invasion and conquest of Britain, with his legions commanded by the Roman general (and first provincial governor) Aulus Plautius. Subsequent campaigns would see most of what is now England and Wales brought under Roman control and fully integrated into the Roman Empire. The next three and a half centuries saw the emergence of a Romano-British culture and society, during which time many of our major towns and cities were established and connected by a Roman road system, which gave access to numerous rural settlements, villas and their estates (Salway 1981).

Religious practices within the province appear to have mirrored those of the wider Roman Empire, and until the early fourth century were largely pagan (polytheistic) and syncretistic. They included the worship of the 'great gods' of the Graeco-Roman pantheon, the cult of the Roman Emperor, various ancestor and mother goddess cults, eastern mysticism (including Mithraism and the cult of Isis) and assimilated native British deities. The last of these categories came about through an established Roman practice known as *interpretatio romana*, with the most well-known example being the goddess *Sulis-Minerva* worshipped at *Aquae-Sulis* the Roman city of Bath (Green 1986). As yet there is no direct evidence of any Jewish presence in Roman Britain, but the existence of individuals or small communities within the province would not be surprising (Applebaum 1951). Christianity on the island is first recorded in the accounts of three British martyrs: St Alban, St Julius and St Aaron, who were most likely put to death during the major persecutions of the third century (Petts 2016, 661). It was in Britain that Constantine was proclaimed emperor by his army at York 306 AD (Salway 1981, 322–324), and with his conversion to Christianity in 312 AD (discussed in the previous chapter) Britain became part of a progressively more Christian Roman empire. Within two years of this event three British bishops (Eborius, Restitutus and Adelphius) attended the synod or Council of Arles in 314 AD (Munier 1963, 15). This was the first council to be called by Constantine and anticipated many of the subjects discussed at the following Council of Nicaea. The council's recommendations or 'canons' were conveyed in a letter (Munier 1963, 4–6) to Pope Sylvester I (reigned 314–335 AD), the first of which concerned the Paschal festival and that it should be observed on the same Sunday by all Christians throughout the world:

> *Primo in loco de observatione paschae dominicae: ut uno die et uno tempore per omnem orbem a nobis observaretur, ut iuxta consuetudinem litteras ad omnes tu dirigas.* In the first place, concerning the celebration of Easter Sunday: that it be observed by us on one day and at one time in all the earth, and that you should send out letters to all, as is the custom. (Munier 1963, 9–13)

Archaeology has revealed significant evidence of Christianity in Roman Britain in the form of portable objects and buildings bearing Christian symbols and imagery. Perhaps the most well-known of these being the silver hoard from Water Newton in Cambridgeshire, the lead tank (font?) from Icklingham in Suffolk, the wall paintings from Lullingstone Roman Villa in Kent, and the mosaic pavement from Hinton St Mary in Dorset (all in the British Museum). Since Constantine's conversion to Christianity it had become the *de facto* official cult of the Roman emperors. Nevertheless, it was not until 380 AD, when Emperor Theodosius I issued the Edict of Thessalonica, that Christianity became the state religion of the Roman Empire (Petts 2016, 1). However, the Empire was by now coming under increasing pressure from external threats on its borders, with Britain having suffered a coordinated attack (by the *Scotti* from Hibernia, the *Picti* from Caledonia, and the *Saxones* from Germania) during the 'Barbarian Conspiracy' of 367 AD (Salway 1981, 375–380). The Roman legions were withdrawn from Britain in 406 AD, and following the sack of Rome by the Visigoths in 410 AD the Emperor Honorius responded to British pleas for military assistance with the *Rescript of Honorius* bidding them to guard themselves (Salway 1981, 415–445). This left the island of Britain vulnerable to further attack and ultimately led to the Anglo-Saxon settlement of lowland Britain (to be discussed in the next chapter).

With the collapse of the provincial Roman government and economy, Britain entered a period (from the fifth to seventh century AD) of internal conflict between competing tyrants and warlords. These leaders were vying with each other for control over native British territories or sub-kingdoms (Salway 1981, 446–501), while at the same time attempting to halt the advancing Anglo-Saxons. The was the period described by the British monk Gildas in *De Excidio Brittaniae* (*The Ruin of Britain*) where he characterises the pagan Saxons ravaging the island 'from sea to sea' as a divine punishment sent by God (Winterbottom 1978, chapter 24).

Nevertheless, Christianity survived within these post-Roman kingdoms of northern and western Britain, as demonstrated by the numerous local saints recorded in Welsh and Cornish place names, and the many inscribed early Christian memorials and stone crosses found within these regions (Morris 1977). These holy men and women included the patron saints of Wales and Ireland, St David and St Patrick, both of whom were British by birth with St Patrick credited with bringing Christianity to Ireland. The paschal festival, with its central themes regarding the forgiveness of sins and the resurrection of the dead, was (and is) the most important annual event in the Christian calendar, and was a time when many converts would have been baptised into the new faith. The Latin festival name *Pascha* was borrowed into Old Welsh as *Pasc* and thence from their British priest and missionaries into Old Irish as *Cásc*, the change in initial consonant reflecting the division between of the Brittonic (P-Celtic) and Goidelic (Q-Celtic) languages (see table 4).

Brittonic (P-Celtic) Languages		Goidelic (Q-Celtic) Languages	
Old Welsh	*Pasc*	Old Irish	*Cásc*
Welsh	*Pasg*	Irish Gaelic	*Cáisc*
Cornish	*Pask*	Scottish Gaelic	*Càisg*
Breton	*Pask*	Manx Gaelic	*Caisht*

Table 4. Paschal (Easter and Passover) festival names in the Celtic language group.

The Latin personal name *Pascentius*—thought to indicate those born during the Paschal season like the French name Pascal (from the Latin *Paschalis*)—also gave rise to Brittonic equivalents (Old Welsh *Pascent* and *Pasken* > Welsh *Pasgen*). Notable examples from the post-Roman period include: PASCENT recorded on a fifth or early sixth-century inscribed stone (now lost) at Towyn Churchyard in Merionethshire (Nash-Williams, 1950, no. 286),

PASCENT son of the fifth-century British king Vortigern, who is recorded by Nennius in the *Historia Brittonum* (Mommsen 1898, 192–193) and on the Pillar of Eliseg at Valle Crucis Abbey in Denbighshire (Nash-Williams, 1950, no. 182), and PASKEN son of the sixth-century king Urien of Rheged (Cumbria) who is recorded in the *Welsh Triads* (Bromwich 1978, nos. 23 and 43).

Thus, we can confidently say that in Roman and Post-Roman Britain the Christian Feast of the Resurrection was known by its Latin name *Pascha*, and by its related insular Celtic (British and Irish) names *Pasc* and *Cásc*, with descendant names still used in all the modern Celtic languages. Furthermore, the timing of this festival was initially set each year by the Church in Rome, and then later calculated by *computus* (using calendric tables and formula) to determine the dates of the Paschal full moon and Resurrection Sunday. With the conversion of Ireland and the export of Irish Christianity to Iona in Scotland by St Columba in 563 AD, these practices were extended to other new monastic centres in northern Britain, including the Holy Island of Lindisfarne (to be discussed in the next chapter).

CHAPTER 3

Eostre to Easter:

The Christian Borrowing of a Pagan Festival Name

In the mid-fifth century AD the Anglo-Saxons—who comprised a number of different, but related, Germanic speaking peoples—began to leave their coastal homelands in northern Germany and Denmark, and to settle in lowland Britain following the collapse of Roman rule. The Angles (Latin *Anglii*) were first recorded in 98 AD by the Roman historian Tacitus in his study of the continental Germanic peoples, the *Germania* (Mattingly, 1970, 134-5). The *Anglii* are thought to have been located in what is now the border area between Germany and Denmark, and where a peninsula on the Baltic Sea coast still bears the name *Angeln*. The Saxons (Latin *Saxones*) were located to the south and west of this area along the North Sea coast in what is today the German region of *Niedersachsen* (Lower Saxony). From the late third century onwards, Roman Britain had been subject to sporadic coastal raiding by the *Saxones* (Salway 1981, 375–380), including their participation in the 'Barbarian Conspiracy' of 367 AD (discussed in the previous chapter). The arrival and settlement of these Germanic peoples in post-Roman Britain is described by the Northumbrian scholar and historian Bede (672–735 AD) in his *Ecclesiastical History of the English People* (King 1930, 1: 68–74). Bede identifies the Angles, Saxons and Jutes (from Jutland) as the principal Germanic peoples who migrated to Britain, and where they settled on the island. In addition to which, these migrants may have included Frisians or *Phrissiones* as identified by the sixth-century Byzantine historian Procopius in his *Gothic Wars* (book 4, chapter 20). The excavation of Anglo-Saxon cemetery sites in England has revealed pottery, weaponry, brooches, and other decorative metalwork that clearly match those found in the continental homelands of these peoples in the Low Countries, northern Germany and Denmark. Furthermore, in the Schleswig Holstein region of northern Germany (including *Angeln*) archaeologists have recognised a major gap in settlement continuity during the migration period, which would appear to support Bede's claim that the homeland of the Angles was left deserted (Welch 1992).

Nevertheless, the nature of the Anglo-Saxon settlement has become a matter of some contention, with arguments often polarised between those supporting a large-scale folk migration, versus those supporting a small dominant elite takeover. Having previously written on this subject (Sermon 2000 and 2003) I believe that the truth has to lie somewhere between the two extremes. There must have been a substantial migration and settlement of Germanic peoples in the post-Roman period in order to establish the cultural and linguistic dominance of the Anglo-Saxons in lowland Britain. However, this must have gone on hand in hand with the assimilation of native populations steadily cut off from the main body of surviving British culture. Recent DNA analysis would now appear to support this view in a genome-wide study of 460 individuals from migration period cemeteries in north-western Europe, including 278 individuals from southern and eastern England (Gretzinger et al. 2022). This study has identified 'a substantial increase of continental northern European ancestry in early medieval England, which is closely related to the early medieval (and present-day) inhabitants of Germany and Denmark, implying large-scale substantial migration across the North Sea into Britain' during this period. The sampled individuals from these Anglo-Saxon cemeteries 'derived up to 76% of their ancestry from the continental North Sea zone', but with a decreasing proportion in the more western cemeteries, such as Worth Matravers in Dorset where the majority had native British ancestry (Gretzinger et al. 2022, figure 8a). This new DNA evidence was the focus of a special issue of *Current Archaeology*, in which John Hines discussed and summarised its broader implications:

> These genetic data turn an uncompromisingly clear spotlight on to arguments that have sought to marginalise or even erase the substance of the changes that affected southern and eastern England at the start of the Anglo-Saxon period, when a largely new material culture was introduced—now undeniably accompanied by the regionally dominant presence of settlers who (and whose ancestors) were at home with that culture. (Hines 2022, 24)

The cultural changes introduced by these migrants included not only a new material culture, in the form of artefacts, burial practice and settlement pattern, but also a new language and new religious beliefs. The Anglo-Saxons spoke a number of mutually intelligible West Germanic dialects known collectively as Old English (450–1150 AD), which through Middle English (1150–1500) is the ancestor of both modern English and Lowland Scots. By the reign of King Athelstan (924–939 AD) the Anglo-Saxons were referring to themselves as the *Englisc*, after the Angles, and using this name to describe their language, culture and homeland *Englaland*. Conversely, the Celtic speaking Britons and Irish referred to them as Saxons, giving rise to the modern Welsh *Saesneg*, Irish *Sasanach* and Scottish Gaelic *Sasunnach* (a term originally applied to both the English and Scottish Lowlanders).

The continental homelands of the Anglo-Saxons lay outside the Roman Empire, and largely outside the influence of early Christianity. Thus, they retained their pagan religious beliefs and practices, and carried these ideas with them across the North Sea to Britain. Their gods, heroes and legends were similar to those of the other Germanic speaking peoples, with the most detailed accounts found in the thirteenth-century literature of medieval Iceland. These Old

Norse myths and sagas are often used to help reconstruct the pagan beliefs of the early Anglo-Saxons, and, while we must exercise caution, there is clearly much agreement suggesting a common origin. The names of their principal deities still cross our lips on a daily basis, although largely unrecognised, in the names given to our days of the week. With the adoption of the Roman seven-day week (whose days were named after the planets) Saturday, Sunday and Monday were named after the same heavenly bodies as their Latin equivalents, while Tuesday, Wednesday, Thursday and Friday were named after the Anglo-Saxon (and wider Germanic) gods *Tiw*, *Woden*, *Þunor* and *Frig*. References to gods and heroes can be found in various Anglo-Saxon manuscripts, which include Old English poems, charms, histories and royal genealogies. They also survive in English place names and in the mythical origins attributed to earlier prehistoric, Roman and post-Roman monuments; two notable examples would include the chambered Neolithic long barrow known as Wayland's Smithy on the Ridgeway in south Oxfordshire, and the linear earthen bank and ditch known as the Wansdyke (Woden's dyke) running between the counties Wiltshire and Somerset (Neidorf 2022).

The Christian missions sent to convert the pagan Anglo-Saxons came from two very different directions, both geographically and culturally. The first was led by St Augustine who was sent to England (Kent) by Pope Gregory the Great in 596 AD. Although suffering many setbacks, this mission would eventually succeed in converting the kings of Kent, Essex, East Anglia and Wessex to Christianity. Following the death of the king Penda at the battle of Winwaed in 655 AD Mercia finally became Christian and Wessex was freed from Mercian control; thus making way for the conversion of Sussex and the Isle of Wight where the last openly pagan king Arwald was killed in battle in 686 AD. Missionaries from the Church of Rome were also sent into Northumbria where Paulinus began to preach and baptise in 625 AD, but following the resurgence of paganism within the kingdom he was forced back to Kent in 633 AD. The following year saw Oswald, who as a youth had been exiled to the Hiberno-Scottish kingdom of *Dál Riata* where he had converted to Christianity, become king of Northumbria. In 635 AD Oswald invited Aidan, from St Columba's monastery on the Scottish island Iona, to begin missionary work among the Northumbrians and to establish a similar monastery on the tidal island of Lindisfarne. Under Aidan's successors, including St Cuthbert (634-687 AD), Christianity was to spread throughout what is now northern England and southern Scotland. This established Irish forms of Christian worship and monasticism in Northumbria, which were in many ways quite distinct and older than those practised to the south under the influence of the Church of Rome. One often quoted example is the different shape of tonsure (shaved scalp) worn by the two monastic traditions, but perhaps the most contentious issue was a disagreement over the formula that should be used to calculate the date of the Paschal (Easter) feast.

Paschal Month (day number)	Roman only	Roman & Irish	Roman & Irish	Roman & Irish	Roman & Irish	Roman & Irish	Roman & Irish	Irish only
07	Sun	Mon	Tue	Wed	Thu	Fri	Sat	Sun (PS)
08	Mon	Tue	Wed	Thu	Fri	Sat	Sun (PS)	Mon
09	Tue	Wed	Thu	Fri	Sat	Sun (PS)	Mon	Tue
10	Wed	Thu	Fri	Sat	Sun (PS)	Mon	Tue	Wed
11	Thu	Fri	Sat	Sun (PS)	Mon	Tue	Wed	Thu
12	Fri	Sat	Sun (PS)	Mon	Tue	Wed	Thu	Fri
13	Sat	Sun (PS)	Mon	Tue	Wed	Thu	Fri	Sat
14 (Full Moon)	Sun (PS)	Mon	Tue	Wed	Thu	Fri	Sat	Sun (RS)
15	Mon	Tue	Wed	Thu	Fri	Sat	Sun (RS)	Mon
16	Tue	Wed	Thu	Fri	Sat	Sun (RS)	Mon	Tue
17	Wed	Thu	Fri	Sat	Sun (RS)	Mon	Tue	Wed
18	Thu	Fri	Sat	Sun (RS)	Mon	Tue	Wed	Thu
19	Fri	Sat	Sun (RS)	Mon	Tue	Wed	Thu	Fri
20	Sat	Sun (RS)	Mon	Tue	Wed	Thu	Fri	Sat
21	Sun (RS)	Mon	Tue	Wed	Thu	Fri	Sat	Sun

Table 5. Showing Palm Sunday (PS) and Resurrection Sunday (RS) agreements between the Roman and Irish methods of *computus*, when the Paschal full moon falls on any day except Sunday (columns 3 to 8), and their disagreement (by one week) when the Paschal full moon falls on a Sunday (columns 2 and 9).

During the mid-seventh century the thorny issue of *computus* (the method of calculating the date of Easter) came to a head in the royal household of Northumbria. King Oswig, who followed the Irish method, had married Eanflæd of Kent (in 642 AD), who followed the Roman method, and many times the royal couple found themselves celebrating the Paschal feast on different dates. Thus in 664 AD the Synod of Whitby was convened at St Hilda's Abbey to investigate and finally resolve the matter, which would eventually bring all the churches in Britain and Ireland into agreement. With Oswig and other nobles and clergy in attendance, it was St Wilfrid (c. 633–710 AD) bishop of York who spoke in support of the Roman method, while Colmán (c. 605–675 AD) bishop of Lindisfarne defended the Irish method. According to Bede, who provides the most detailed account of the proceedings (King 1930, 1: 461–477), the main difference between the two methods was whether Resurrection Sunday could fall 'on or after' the Paschal full moon (the Irish method), or could only fall 'after' the Paschal full moon (the Roman method):

> Roman Computus: The Paschal new moon is the first day of the Paschal month, and its fourteenth day reckoned to be the Paschal full moon (on or after the ecclesiastical vernal equinox), RESPECTING the nineteen lunar-year (Metonic) cycle. Resurrection Sunday is reckoned to be the first Sunday AFTER the Paschal full moon, and thus falls between the FIFTEENTH and TWENTY-FIRST day of the Paschal month.

> Irish Computus: The Paschal new moon is the first day of the Paschal month, and its fourteenth day reckoned to be the Paschal full moon (on or after the ecclesiastical vernal equinox), IRRESPECTIVE of the nineteen lunar-year (Metonic) cycle. Resurrection Sunday is reckoned to be the first Sunday ON or AFTER the Paschal full moon, and thus falls between the FOURTEENTH and TWENTIETH day of the Paschal month.

A discrepancy between the two methods of *computus* appears to have occurred when the Paschal full moon fell on a Sunday (see table 5, columns 2 and 9), and when the followers of the Roman method (including Queen Eanflæd) would have been celebrating Palm Sunday (and fasting during Lent) the followers of the Irish method (including King Oswig) would have been celebrating Resurrection Sunday (and the Paschal feast). The potential for these disagreements within Northumbrian court would have lasted from Oswig's marriage to Eanflæd in 642 AD until the Synod of Whitby in 664 AD (see table 6), when the authority of the Church of Rome was accepted on this and other matters.

Year AD	19 Lunar Year (Metonic) Cycle	Paschal Full Moon (date)	Paschal Month (day number)	Resurrection Sunday (date)	Paschal Month (day number)
642	13	21 March	14	24 March	17
643	14	9 April	14	13 April	19
644	15	29 March	14	4 April	20
645 *	16	17 April	14	24 April	21
646	17	5 April	14	9 April	18
647 *	18	25 March	14	1 April	21
648 *	19	13 April	14	20 April	21
649	1	2 April	14	5 April	17
650	2	22 March	14	28 March	20
651 *	3	10 April	14	17 April	21
652	4	30 March	14	1 April	16
653	5	18 April	14	21 April	17
654	6	7 April	14	13 April	20
655	7	27 March	14	29 March	16
656	8	15 April	14	17 April	16
657	9	4 April	14	9 April	19
658	10	24 March	14	25 March	15
659	11	12 April	14	14 April	16
660	12	1 April	14	5 April	18
661 *	13	21 March	14	28 March	21
662	14	9 April	14	10 April	15
663	15	29 March	14	2 April	18
664	16	17 April	14	21 April	18

Table 6. Extract from Bede's Paschal Table (after Wallis 1999, 394–395, Appendix 2) employing the Roman method of *computus*. Asterisks indicate years when those following the Irish method of *computus* would have observed the Paschal feast one week earlier: on the date of the Paschal full moon (day 14 of the Paschal month).

Unlike their Celtic speaking neighbours the Anglo-Saxons used a very different name for the Paschal festival, with what may be the earliest reference to 'Easter' or *Eastran* (Attenborough 1922, 54–55, law 55) found in the laws of King Ine of Wessex (reigned 688–726 AD): *Ewo bið mid hire giunge sceape scill[ingas] weorð oþþæt XII niht ofer Eastran* 'A ewe with her young sheep (lamb) is worth a shilling until twelve nights after Easter' (Cambridge, Corpus Christi College, MS 173, f.51r). King Ine's laws were written in Old English and appended to those of the later, and more famous, King Alfred of Wessex. However, it has recently been argued that Ine's laws were originally composed in Latin, and only translated into Old English and attached to Alfred's laws in the late ninth century (Ivarsen 2022). Nevertheless, the more securely dated laws of King Wihtræd of Kent, issued during the sixth year of his reign (c. 690–725 AD), contain a law against trespass (Attenborough 1922, 30–31, law 28) that is almost identical to one of Ine's laws (Attenborough 1922, 42–43, law 20), thus suggesting that both Old English texts share a similar late seventh-century date of composition, with the presented counterarguments appearing somewhat contrived and convoluted (Ivarsen 2022, note 14).

The earliest explanation for the Easter festival name was provided by the Venerable Bede (c. 673–735 AD), the great Northumbrian scholar and English historian, at St Peter's monastery in Jarrow. In a comprehensive and detailed work, entitled *De Temporum Ratione* (The Reckoning of Time) and completed in 725 AD, he explained the motions of the sun and the moon and their influences on the changing seasons, day lengths, lunar phases and marine tides (Jones 1977; Wallis 1999). He also described and discussed various ancient calendars including those of the Hebrews, Egyptians, Romans and Greeks. However, it was the vexed subject of *computus* that was his primary concern, and the methods used to determine the dates of the lunar 'movable feasts' (those tied to and including Resurrection Sunday), and their positions in relation to the solar 'fixed feasts' of the ecclesiastical year. Yet following his discussion of the ancient

Greek calendar Bede introduces what may have been something of an afterthought—'for it did not seem fitting to me that I should speak of other nations' observance of the year and yet be silent about my own' (Wallis 1999, 54)—when he describes the pagan Anglo-Saxon year. Bede tells us that the year consisted of twelve lunar months (and one intercalary month), which could be approximated to those of the solar Julian calendar (see table 7), and described what he believed to be the meanings and origins of the Old English month

Bede's Month Name	West Saxon Name	Translation	Roman Equivalent
Giuli	Æfterra Geola	Later Yule	January
Solmonath	Solmonað	Sol-month	February
Rhedmonath	Hreðmonað	Hreth-month	March
Eosturmonath	Eastermonað	Easter-month	April
Thrimilchi	Ðrimilce	Three-milkings	May
Lida	Ærra Liða	Earlier Litha	June
Lida	Æfterra Liða	Later Litha	July
Weodmonath	Weodmonað	Weed-month	August
Halegmonath	Haligmonað	Holy-month	September
Winterfilleth	Winterfylleð	Winter-full-moon	October
Blodmonath	Blotmonað	Blood-month	November
Giuli	Ærra Geola	Earlier Yule	December

Table 7. Bede's Old English month names (*Caput XV. De Mensibus Anglorum*).

names. The year began at *Giuli* (Yule) on 25 December, then reckoned to be the date of the winter solstice as well as the Feast of the Nativity (Christmas) and was preceded by a festival known as *Modra Nect* (Mothers' Night). *Guili* was not only the name for midwinter, but also for the months before and after the solstice. This was followed by *Solmonath* (Mud-month?) when cakes were offered to the gods. The following two months (equated with March and April) were said to have been named after the goddesses *Rheda* and *Eostre*, who were each celebrated in their respective months. *Eostre* gave her name to *Eosturmonth* (Easter-month), which by Bede's time had taken on a new Christian meaning as the name for the Paschal month and season:

Eosturmonath, qui nunc paschalis mensis interpretatur, quondam a dea illorum quae Eostre vocabatur, et cui in illo festa celebrabant, nomen habuit, a cuius nomine nunc paschale tempus cognominant, consueto antiquae observationis vocabulo gaudia novae solemnitatis vocantes. (Jones 1977, 330–331)

Eosturmonath has a name which is now translated 'Paschal month', and which was once called after a goddess of theirs named *Eostre*, in whose honour feasts were celebrated in that month. Now they designate that Paschal season by her name, calling the joys of the new rite by the time-honoured name of the old observance. (Wallis 1999, 54)

Then came the month of *Thrimilchi* (Three-milkings) when the land was so bountiful that their cattle had to be milked three times a day. Halfway through the year was midsummer or *Lida* (Litha), which like *Giuli* was flanked by two months bearing the same name. *Weodmonath* (Weed-month) was simply the month weeds were most abundant, and *Halegmonath* (Holy-month) when sacred rites were held. Finally came *Winterfilleth* the first full moon of winter, and *Blodmonath* (Blood-month) when animals were slaughtered and offerings made to the gods. Bede records these month names in his own Northumbrian dialect of Old English, but West Saxon versions of them exist in a number of ninth to early eleventh-century sources; most notably in Byrhtferth of Ramsey's *Enchiridion* (Crawford 1929, 25), a vernacular handbook or manual of *computus*, and in an *Old English Martyrology*, where in spite of a missing section covering most of *Solmonað* the month names are all listed (Herzfel 1900, 12, 32, 52, 68, 88, 110, 132, 160, 184, 198 and 216). In addition to which the terms *ærra* (earlier) and *æftera* (later) appear before and after the double month names *Geola* and *Liða*.

Old English	Latin (Bede)	Modern Equivalent
Lencten	Ver	Spring
Sumor	Aestas	Summer
Hærfest	Autumnus	Autumn (Fall)
Winter	Hiems	Winter
Middansumor	–	Midsummer
Middanwinter	–	Midwinter
Lenctenlice Emnihte	Aequinoctium Vernale	Spring Equinox
Sumorlica Sunstede	Solstitium Aestivale	Summer Solstice
Hærfestlice Emnihte	Aequinoctium Autumnale	Autumn Equinox
Winterlica Sunstede	Solstitium Hiemale	Winter Solstice

Table 8. Anglo-Saxon (Old English) season, solstice and equinox names.

Bede goes on to explain that the pagan Anglo-Saxon year was originally divided into just two seasons: Winter and Summer. The earliest references to *Lencten* (Spring) and *Hærfest* (Autumn/Fall) occur in ninth-century texts, and logically described the seasons when days began to lengthen, and when the crops were harvested (see table 8). These seasonal names survive as the modern religious and secular terms for Lent (the Christian fast before Easter) and Harvest time. In Byrhtferth's *Enchiridion* all four seasons are described as *þa feower timan amearcod: lengten, sumor, hærfest & winter* (Crawford 1929, 10), and are similarly listed in Ælfric of Eynsham's *De Temporibus Anni*, a vernacular paraphrase of Bede's work on time (Henel 1942, 36). While Bede discusses various dates on which the seasons were reckoned to have commenced, he suggests that the solstices and equinoxes marked the midpoints of the four seasons (Wallis 1999, 101-102). This is clearly borne out by the Old English summer and winter solstice names *middansumor* (midsummer) and *middanwinter* (midwinter), and by Byrhtferth's correlation between the Latin and native English terms: *þæt ys on Lyden solstitium & on Englisc midsumor* (Crawford 1929, 86). In contrast, the solstice

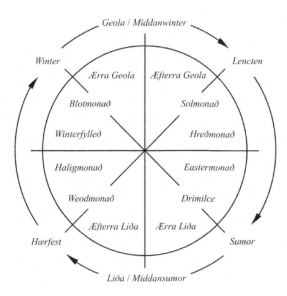

Figure 1. Diagrammatic reconstruction of the Anglo-Saxon year based on surviving Old English sources (drawn by the author).

and equinox names used by Ælfric appear to be loan-translations (or calques) of Bede's Latin terminology (Henel 1942, 38 and 46), as do the equinox names used by Byrhtferth (Crawford 1929, 136):

Latin *sol* + *stitium* > Old English *sun* + *stede*
Latin *aequi* + *noctium* > Old English *em* + *nihte*

Thus, it is unknown whether any earlier Old English names for the equinoxes had existed.

Nevertheless, from this brief survey of the principal sources it is possible to establish the major divisions (months, seasons and solstices) of the pagan Anglo-Saxon year (see figure 1), many of which have survived into modern English usage, and are found throughout the Germanic language group (see table 9).

English	Low Saxon	Dutch	German	Swedish
Yule	–	–	–	Jul
Lent	–	Lente	Lenz	Vår
Easter	Oostern	–	Ostern	–
Summer	Sommer	Zomer	Sommer	Sommar
Midsummer	Midsommer	Midzomer	Mittsommer	Midsommar
Harvest	Harvst	Herfst	Herbst	Höst
Winter	Winter	Winter	Winter	Vinter
Midwinter	Midwinter	Midwinter	Mittwinter	Midvinter
Old English	**Old Saxon**	**Middle Dutch**	**Old High German**	**Old Norse**
Geola	–	–	–	Jól
Lencten	–	Lentin	Lengizin	Vár
Eastron	Asteron?	–	Ostarun	–
Sumor	Sumar	Somer	Sumar	Sumar
Middansumor	Middensumar	Midsomer	Mittesumar	Miðsumar
Hærfest	Herfst	Herfst	Herbist	Haust
Winter	Wintar	Winter	Wintar	Vetr
Middanwinter	Middenwintar	Midwinter	Mittewintar	Miðvetr

Table 9. Common Germanic season and festival names (with early and modern examples).

While the existence of a pagan Anglo-Saxon calendar (with its named lunar months) has largely remained unchallenged, by the latter half of the twentieth century many academics began to question the reliability of Bede's explanations of the Old English month names. By way of example, Ronald Hutton suggests that Bede had only sketchy knowledge of the practices he described, that 'Mothers Night' could in fact refer to a celebration of the Virgin Mary on the eve of the Nativity, and that it was not until the eleventh century that 'Danish rule over England resulted in the introduction of the colloquial Scandinavian term for Christmas, Yule' (Hutton, 1996, 6). He also suggests that *Eosturmonath* could simply refer to an opening or beginning month, as the name is cognate with the East and the dawn sky (Hutton, 1996, 180). However, it is important to note that although Yule is cognate with the Old Norse festival *Jól* and winter month *Ýlir*, Bede was writing about *Giuli* in the early eighth century AD, almost seventy years before the first Viking raid on Lindisfarne in 793 AD, and 140 years before the first Danish settlement in England in 865 AD. Furthermore, in the laws of King Alfred of Wessex (reigned 871–899 AD) we find references to both *Gehhol* and *Eastron* (Attenborough 1922, 66–67 and 84–85, laws 5.5 and 43), at a time when Old Norse was yet to have any significant influence on West Saxon vocabulary.

Nevertheless, it is Bede's origin of *Eosturmonath* that has been the subject of most academic criticism, with these doubts now being reflected in wider reference publications (Simpson and Roud 2000, 103; Roud 2008, 140). In the English-speaking world these doubts have tended to focus on whether Bede's use of *Eostre* as a theophoric explanation for the month name was simply conjecture—particularly when the preceding *Rhedmonath* is said to have been named after *Rheda*, another goddess for whom there is little or no supporting evidence. However, there may be a very simple reason for this lack of evidence. It is quite possible that Bede's information did not come from any written source, but from the personal knowledge or recollections of the people he knew, including members of his own family:

> Suspect though some of Bede's etymology may be, and allusive as

some of his information is, it is none the less likely that this passage is a first-class record of the festal aspects of English paganism which it treats; it is possible that Bede's father and almost certain that his grandfather could remember the heyday of Northumbrian heathenism. (Mayr-Harting 1991, 22)

Furthermore, as a devout Christian scholar and historian—whose most well-known work was concerned with the history of the English people and their conversion to Christianity—'it seems unlikely that Bede would have invented a fictitious pagan festival [and goddess] in order to account for a Christian one' (Green 2000, 353; *Oxford English Dictionary* 2022). From what seems to be its earliest occurrence in late seventh-century laws of King Ine of Wessex, to its use in the tenth-century glosses added to the *Lindisfarne Gospels* (Cook 1894, 44), *Eastron* became the established Old English name for the Paschal festival. Nevertheless, it is important to recognise that, with the exception of Bede's single reference to *Eostre*, the Old English name always referred to either the Christian or Jewish festivals, and not to any early Anglo-Saxon pagan tradition (Parker 2022, 126-127). Although later challenged by the introduction of the Norman French name *Pasche*, the Middle English name *Eastren* would ultimately prevail and give rise to the modern English name EASTER. While the native festival name had survived through the medieval period, Bede's explanation for the name appears to have gone largely unnoticed in England until the late sixteenth century, when the antiquarian and historian William Camden (1551–1623) included it in his major work *Britannia*:

> *Eoster* etiam Deam habuerunt, cui mense Aprili sacrificarunt, unde Aprilem, inquit Beda in libro de temporibus, *Eoster monath* vocarunt, et nos paschatis festum etiamnum *Eoster* vocamus. (Camden 1586, 48)

> They had a Goddesse also named *Eoster*, unto whom they sacrificed in the moneth of Aprill: and hence it commeth, saith Beda [marginal note: *De temporibus*], that they called Aprill,

Eoster monath, and we still name the feast of the Resurrection, *Eoster*; but rather as I think of the rising of Christ, which our progenitors called East, as we do now that part whence the Sunne riseth. (Camden 1610, 135)

First published in Latin in 1586, Camden's discussion of *Eostre* may have been influenced by existing Swiss and German references to Bede's work (Münster 1550, 45; Herwagen 1563, 81), which are explored in the next chapter. Nevertheless, the 1610 English edition of his *Britannia* (translated by Philemon Holland) contained numerous additions by Camden, including what appears to be the first suggested connection between Easter, the East, and the position of the rising sun—albeit as an allusion to 'the rising of Christ'. The translated passage on *Eostre* was almost immediately copied by the English cartographer and historian John Speed (1551–1629) in his *History of Great Britaine* (Speed 1611, 288), and appears in Sir Isaac Newton's (1642–1727) rough notes for his unfinished *Theologiae Gentilis Origines Philosophicae* (Jerusalem, National Library of Israel, Yahuda MS 16.1, f.22r):

> Hence also came the Goddes of ye ancient Saxons *Aestar* or Easter to whom they sacrificed in the month of April which from her was thence: called in their language [*Beda in libro de temporibus*] Easter *monath* as Beda writes... and hence also the English still call the feast of ye Passover Easter.

Following its airing in these early modern sources, Bede's explanation of the festival name would be repeated in numerous English language publications through to the present day.

CHAPTER 4

Ostern to Ostara:

The Reinvention of a Germanic Goddess?

As we have observed in chapter one, in most European languages the Christian Feast of the Resurrection (Paschal festival) has a name that is ultimately derived from the Hebrew word *Pesach* for the week of the Jewish Passover, when Jesus was said to have been crucified and resurrected. However, in English and German the Paschal festival goes by the altogether different names of Easter and *Ostern* (see table 10). The earliest example of the German festival name is found in an Old High German theological glossary named the *Abrogans* after its first entry, and now held in the library of St Gall in Switzerland. This late eighth-century work is significant in being the earliest known book in the German language, and is often attributed to Arbeo who was bishop of Freising in Bavaria from 764 to 783 AD. In the *Abrogans* the author was attempting to translate various Christian concepts and terms into the vernacular language of southern Germany, with the Latin *Pasca* and *Pascua* [sic] interpreted as *Ostarun* in Old High German (St Gallen, Stiftsbibliothek, MS 911, 226).

Our next example comes from the reign of Charlemagne (742–814 AD), king of the Franks and founder of the Holy Roman Empire. In Einhard's early ninth-century *Vita Karoli Magni* (Life of Charlemagne) he describes how Charlemagne finally defeated the continental Saxons and converted them to Christianity; and as part of his reforms (chapter 29) gave new Germanic names to the Latin months of the year (Dutton 1998, 34), many of which went on to survive into early modern German (Runde 1781, 8–9). How far these month names were completely new, or based on earlier pre-Christian names is difficult to say. Nevertheless, Charlemagne's new Frankish name for April was *Ostarmanoth* (see table 11), which is clearly cognate with Bede's *Eosturmonath*.

Language	Name	Language	Name
Old English	Eastron	Old High German	Ostarun
Middle English	Eastren	Middle High German	Osteren
Modern English	Easter	Modern German	Ostern

Table 10. Stages in the development of the English and German Paschal festival names.

Frankish Name	Interpretation	Traditional Names	Roman Equivalent
Wintarmanoth	Winter-month	Wintermonat	January
Hornung	Irregular-month?	Hornung	February
Lenzinmanoth	Spring-month	Lenzmonat	March
Ostarmanoth	Easter-month	Ostermonat	April
Winnemanoth	Pasture-month	Wonnemonat	May
Brachmanoth	Fallow-month	Brachmonat	June
Hewimanoth	Hay-month	Heumonat	July
Aranmanoth	Harvest-month	Erntemonat	August
Witumanoth	Wood-month	Herbstmonat	September
Windumemanoth	Wine-month	Weinmonat	October
Herbistmanoth	Autumn-month	Windmonat	November
Heilagmanoth	Holy-month	Heiligenmonat	December

Table 11. Charlemagne's Frankish month names and their surviving traditional names.

By the mid to late ninth century the German festival name would seem to have become reasonably well established and appears in two Old High German gospel harmonies. The first is a translation of Tatian's second-century *Diatessaron*, where the fes-

40

tival name appears repeatedly as either *Ostron* or *Ostrun* (Sievers 1892, 30, 160, 204–205, 230–231, 233–234, 259 and 264); the second is Otfrid von Weissenburg's *Evangelienbuch* (1:22:4, 3:4:1 and 4:9:4), which provides examples of the name in three of its rhyming couplets (Graff 1831, 79, 182 and 292):

Wir forahtlicho iz weizen, ioh Ostoron heizen.
We bear witness with awe, and Passover it is called. (see Luke 2:41)

Thio ziti sih bibrahtun, thaz Ostoron tho nahtun.
Some time later, that was the eve of Passover. (see John 5:1)

Gibot thaz sies gizilotin, thie Ostoron in gigarotin.
He bid that they strive, to prepare the Passover. (see Luke 21:8)

In addition to the Old High German name there is evidence for a possible Old Low German (Old Saxon) equivalent *Asteron*. It appears in the *Freckenhorster Heberegister*, an eleventh-century ledger of monastic supplies, which contains an intriguing entry: *Ande to themo asteron-hus uif gerstena malt gimelta* 'And to the *asteron-hus* five measures (*malter*) of malted barley' (Staatsarchiv Münster, MS VII, 1316a). The term *asteron-hus* could refer to either an 'Eastern-house' of the monastery, or an 'Easter-house' (Paschal-house) where supplies for the Paschal feast were perhaps stored (Hessmann 2000). The latter interpretation is paralleled in the Flemish place name and surname *Paashuis* or *Paeschhuis*, also meaning 'Easter-house', of which the earliest known example is *Paeshuys* recorded at Antwerp in 1386 (Debrabandere 1993, 1073).

The origin of the festival name has also been the subject of much debate in Germany; notably since 1835 when Jacob Grimm (the famous German linguist and folklorist) proposed that the Old High German festival and month names (*Ostarun* and *Ostarmanoth*) must, like their Old English equivalents (*Eastron* and

Eosturmonath), have derived from Bede's goddess *Eostre* (Grimm 1835, 180–182; Stallybrass 1882, 1, 288–291). In his monumental study *Deutsche Mythologie* (Teutonic Mythology) he reconstructed the goddess' Germanic name as '*Ostara*' and highlighted that the origin of both the English and German festival names was a shared linguistic root meaning 'east' or 'eastern'. Given that the sun rises in the east he concluded that *Eostre/Ostara* was the ancient Germanic goddess of the radiant dawn:

> *Ostara, Eastre mag also gottheit des strahlenden morgens, des aufsteigenden lichts gewesen sein, eine freudige, heilbringende erscheinung, deren begrif leicht für das auferstehungsfest des christlichen gottes verwandt werden konnte.* (Grimm 1835, 182)

> Ostara, Eastre seems therefore to have been the divinity of the radiant dawn, of upspringing light, a spectacle that brings joy and blessing, whose meaning could be easily adapted to the resurrection-day of the Christian God. (Stallybrass 1882, 1, 291)

Grimm also noted that the Old High German and Old English festival names (*Ostarun* and *Eastron*) generally appear in their plural forms, suggesting that this reflects the two most important days of the festival marking the crucifixion (Good Friday) and the resurrection (Easter Sunday), also known in Old High German as the *Ostartaga* or 'Easter-days' (Grimm 1835, 181; Stallybrass 1882, 1, 290).

In this chapter we will go on to discuss various criticisms of Grimm's work, but before doing so it is worth asking whether Grimm's thoughts on this subject were all his own work, or was he perhaps building on ideas that had already been circulating in Germany for some time? In his initial paragraph Grimm directly quotes Bede's words on *Eostre* and *Eosturmonath* found in *De Temporum Ratione* (see previous chapter). However, in a footnote to this quote he describes another (hitherto unknown) 'manuscript' suggesting that the goddess *Eostre* was originally worshipped by all the 'Teutonic' peoples:

> Nach einer hs. (Kolmesen opusc. p. 287, dies citat gibt Rathlefs
> Hoya u. Diepholz 3, 16.): *Veteres Anglicani populi vocant Estor-*
> *monath paschalem mensem, idque a dea quadam, cui Teutonici*
> *populi in paganismo sacrificia fecerunt tempore mensis Aprilis, quae*
> *Eostra est appellata.* (Grimm, 1835, 180)

> In another ms. (Kolmesen's works p. 287, this citation given in
> Rathlef's Hoya and Diepholz 3, 16): The ancient English people
> called Estormonath the paschal month after a goddess, to whom
> the Teutonic people in Pagan times made sacrifices in the month
> of April, who is named Eostra. (author's translation)

Of the sources given by Grimm, 'Kolmesen' is initially somewhat
difficult to locate, while Ernst Rathlef is much easier to find. In
his 'Lecture regarding the Worship of the Saxon Goddess Eostra
on the Osterberg near Nienburg' Rathlef quotes the same 'variant'
text and principal source (Rathlef 1766, 16–17); to which he adds
that it was printed in the Hamburg edition of Kolmesen's works
and is from an unpublished version (manuscript) of Bede's *De
Temporum Ratione*. However, based on a repeated and incorrect
page reference (p. 287) this does not appear to be a direct quote
from 'Kolmesen', but to have been copied from the work of Johann
Grimm, a printer and publisher in Bremen (Grimm 1725, 477–
478) who in turn names the unknown source as 'Colomesio' and
states that the 'variant' text came from a manuscript that Glarean
had sent to Basel in 1545, and is preserved in Sebastian Münster's
Cosmographia. The 'Kolmesen' or 'Colomesio' source is without
doubt Paul Colomies, a French Protestant (Huguenot) refugee and
scholar in London, who reproduced a much longer paragraph
found in Münster's *Cosmographia* (Colomies 1688, 220–221,
1709, 688–687), from which Jacob Grimm's 'variant' text is ultimately derived:

> *Anglica lingua mixta est ex multis linguis, praefertim Germanica et*

Gallica. Olim vero mere fuit Germanica, id quod advertere licet ex Beda, qui ex Anglia oriundus fuit: is enim in libro quae de temporibus edidit sicscribit. **Veteres Anglicani populi** *numeraverunt menses suos secundum cursum lunae, appellantque lunam mona (Germani enim vocant lunam mon) et mensem monath. Decembrem* **vocant** *Halegmonath (id est, sacrum mensem) & aprilem* **Eostermonath** *(id est,* **paschalem mensem)** **idque a dea quadam, cui Teutonici populi in paganismo sacrificia fecerunt tempore mensis aprilis, quae Eostre est appellata.** *Maium appellauerunt Thrimelci (id est, tres mulctre) quia in maio ter per dien mulserunt peocora. Hic locus in impressis codicibus non facile invenitur, ego vero inveni in libro manuscripto, quem Glareanus ex nigro sylva anno 1545 huc Basileam misit.* (Münster 1550, 45)

The English language is a mixture of many languages, especially German and French. But once it was purely Germanic, which we may observe from Bede, who was born in England: for he demonstrates this in a book which he wrote concerning time. **The ancient English people** counted their months according to the course of the moon, and called the moon *mona* (for the Germans call the moon *mon*) and the month *monath*. They **called** December *Halegmonath* (that is, the sacred month) and April *Eostermonath* (that is, **the paschal month**) **after a Goddess, to whom the Teutonic people in Pagan times made sacrifices in the month of April, who is named** *Eostre*. They called May *Thrimelci* (that is, three milkings) because in May they milked the cows three times a day. This passage is not easily found in printed codices, but I am sure that it was found in a manuscript book which Glarean sent from the Black Forest to Basel in 1545. (author's translation)

Sebastian Münster (1488–1552) was a German cartographer and professor at the University of Basel. His most famous work was the *Cosmographia*, which sold throughout Europe with many revisions and later reprints. In the 1550 editions (published in Latin and then German) Münster summarised Bede's description of the Old English months (while focusing on *Halegmonath*, *Eostermonath* and *Thrimelci*) and introduced the idea that *Eostre* was not only worshipped by the ancient English (Anglo-Saxons), but by all the Teutonic (Germanic-speaking) peoples. However, this summary was later misunderstood to be Münster quoting an unpublished variant version of Bede's *De Temporum Ratione*. This was largely due to the summary's last sentence (see above quote and translation), which stated that 'this passage' was not easily found in the printed editions of Bede's work, and was thought to have been found in a manuscript that Heinrich Glarean had sent to Basel from Freiburg in 1545.

At the time Münster was writing only two printed editions of *De Temporum Ratione* were available (Flugel 1903, 25–27). The first was edited by Johann Sichard and printed in Basel by Heinrich Petri in 1529, but significantly did not include the chapter *De Mensibus Anglorum* (The English Months). The second was edited by Johann Bronchorst of Neumagen and printed in Cologne in 1537, but could not have been Münster's source as it incorrectly transcribed both the month and goddess names *Costurmonath* [*sic*] and *Cosdre* [*sic*] (Bronchorst 1537, chapter 15). It was not until 1563 that a complete and correct version of the Bede's text was available, edited and printed by Johann Herwagen of Basel (Herwagen 1563, 81), some thirteen years after Münster's 1550 edition of the *Cosmographia*. Thus, the manuscript that Glarean had sent to Basel in 1545 would appear to have been the source of Münster's information. However, this same manuscript may also have been Herwagen's primary source for his printing of *De Temporum Ratione*, which, although completed in 1563 by Johann Herwagen the Younger (died 1564), was begun by his father Johann Herwagen the Elder (died 1557). In this edition each of Bede's chapters are accompanied by glosses attributed to Byrhtferth of Ramsey, which have not been found in any surviving manuscript (Gorman 1996, 209). We know that Glarean (1488–1563) corresponded with the

Herwagens on a number of occasions, including a response to criticism of his ancient *Chronology* where 'Glarean defended himself
in a text directed to the Basel printer Johannes Herwagen in 1555'
(Grafton and Leu 2013, 278). We also known that the Herwagen
had previously collaborated with Münster, including work on the
world map and related description for the *Novus Orbis* (by Johann
Huttich and Simon Grynaeus) published in 1532. With clear connections between these three individuals (Glarean, Herwagen and
Münster) it is not beyond reason to suggest that they were all
linked to the same (now lost) manuscript, which, based on Herwagen's edition, contained Bede's known standard text (Jones
1977). Therefore, in the last sentence of Münster summary 'this
passage' (*hic locus*) is almost certainly referring to Bede's original
chapter (*De Mensibus Anglorum*), rather than Münster's approxi-
mation of it, which:

> (a) mistakenly aligns *Halegmonath* with December rather that
> September, most likely influenced by the Frankish *Heilagma-
> noth* (December) recorded in Einhard's *Vita Karoli Magni* (chap-
> ter 29), and

> (b) includes the line *cui teutonici populi in paganismo sacrificia
> fecerunt* (to whom the Teutonic people in Pagan times made sac-
> rifices), which Bede is unlikely to have written at a time when
> half of Germany was still pagan. (Schaz 1803, 34–35).

Having established the origin and genealogy of Grimm's pan-Germanic goddess theory, we now turn to her reconstructed (indicated by the leading asterisk) name *Ostara (Grimm 1835, 181;
Stallybrass 1882, 290), which again has roots in earlier German
academic literature. Her immediate precursor is *Ostera, the goddess name used by Grimm's known source Ernst Rathlef, who
believed her to have been worshipped on the Osterberg summit
near Nienburg in Lower Saxony (Rathlef 1766, 10). However,
Rathlef's ideas seem to have been drawn from the earlier work of
Luneberg Mushard (Rathlef 1766, 8), a historian and vice-rector

of the cathedral school in Bremen. In Mushard's book *De Ostera Saxonum* (concerning *Ostera* of the Saxons) he makes reference to even earlier seventeenth-century sources (Mushard 1702, 12), including Johann Vorburg's *Historia Romano-Germanica* and Johannes Schild's *De Caucis, Nobilissimo Veteris Germaniae*, both of which discuss Bede's passage on *Eostre* and reconstruct the Germanic goddess name as *Oostera and *Ooster (Vorburg 1659, 32; Schild 1649, 118). However, Mushard's earliest source for the reconstructed goddess name is Clüver's *Germaniae Antiquae* published in 1616. Philipp Clüver (1580-1622) was a German geographer and historian who was born in Danzig (modern Gdańsk) but spent much of his life working in the city of Leiden. He travelled to England where he married and had a son (in Southwark), and, for a time, shared lodgings at Exeter College, Oxford (Wood, 1691, 406–407). Following his return to Holland in 1611 he completed his great work on German Antiquity, which included: a comparison of the initial diphthongs (double vowel sounds) in Easter and *Oostern* (Low German), a discussion of Bede's goddess *Eostre*, and what appears to be the earliest attempt to reconstruct her Germanic name *Ostar (Clüver 1616, 237).

While the points made in the previous paragraphs may appear somewhat laboured, it is important to note that there is no direct evidence for there ever having been a pan-Germanic cult to a goddess named *Ostara*. The many assertions to the contrary found in modern sources will invariably lead back to the work of Jacob Grimm (1823), which can ultimately be traced back to assertions made by Sebastian Münster (1550) and Philip Clüver (1616): that Bede's goddess *Eostre* was worshipped by all the Teutonic (Germanic-speaking) peoples and whose name could be reconstructed as *Oostera or *Ostara. Since the Second World War the work of Jacob Grimm (and other German folklorists) has been widely criticised and deconstructed. Yet, despite the absence of any supporting evidence for his reconstructed goddess *Ostara*, rival theories put forward by modern German linguists are no less problematic. While these theories have proposed alternative routes by which the Paschal festival name *Ostarun* could have arisen in Old High German, they have not adequately explained how the related festival name *Eastron* also arose in Old English.

The first serious challenge to Grimm suggested that the Old High German festival name *Ostarun* was the result of a mistranslation (Knobloch, 1959). In the early church the week following Easter was known in Latin as *hebdomada in albis* (week in white) and sometimes simply as *albae* (white), because the newly baptised Christians would wear their white baptismal robes during that week. However, in Late Latin and the Romance languages this word gained the additional meaning 'dawn' (Italian/Spanish *alba* and French *aube*). Based on this evidence Johann Knoblech (1959, 42–44) argued that when the early German clerics first encountered the Latin word *albae* it was: (a) mistaken for its plural form *alba*, (b) interpreted as meaning 'dawns' rather than 'whites', and (c) then equated with the Old High German word (plural) *ostarun*. However, as noted by other commentators (Green 2000, 352–353; Shaw 2011, 50), this is very tenuous argument based a hypothetical misunderstanding and mistranslation of *alba*, which is then unjustly given priority over Bede's early testimony.

In 1999 Jürgen Udolph, a linguist then at the University of Leipzig, devoted a whole book to his theory that the modern festival name *Ostern* is related to a North Germanic word *ausa* meaning to draw, scoop or pour water. This word is found throughout the Germanic language group, as in the Swedish phrase *ösa en båt* 'bale out a boat', but is now a dialect word in most of the West Germanic languages. A pagan form of baptism for naming newborn children was known in Old Norse as *vatni ausa* 'sprinkling with water'. Based on this evidence Udolph suggests that *Ostern* derives from a common Proto-Germanic root **aus-a*, which in Old High German was applied to the Christian act of baptism. Pointing to central role that baptism played in the Paschal celebrations of the first centuries AD, he argues that the word then became associated with the Paschal festival itself, and appeared in its plural form because it reflected the threefold baptism of the Holy Trinity (see table 12).

Proto-Germanic	Old High German	Modern German
*aus-a- > *aus-r- > *aus-tr- >	*ostr- > ostarun (plural) >	ostern

Table 12. Suggested development of the German name Ostern (after Udolph 1999).

However, whilst it is theoretically possible to project back the Old Norse *ausa* and Old High German *Ostarun* to a common Proto-Germanic root, apart from Old Norse we have no evidence that words derived from this root were used to mean 'baptism' in any of the other Germanic languages. Christian baptism was known in Old Norse by names *deypa* (dip) or *skíra* (cleanse), and Easter by the name *Páskar*, none of which derive from the Proto-Germanic root *aus-a*. Furthermore, it is only in Old Norse that the verb *ausa* means 'to pour'. Elsewhere in the Germanic language group words deriving from the same root have the meaning 'to draw' or 'to scoop'. It should also be noted that our only evidence for the pagan baptism *vatni ausa* comes from Icelandic manuscripts of thirteenth century date or later, which may themselves have been influenced by the Christian baptism following the conversion of Iceland in 1000 AD. As a result, the existence of this pagan water rite is no more certain than is Bede's goddess *Eostre*. Furthermore, in the late eighth-century *Abrogans* the Latin terms *babtismus* (baptism) and *Pasca* (Easter) are equated with *tauffi* and *Ostarun* in Old High German (St Gallen, Stiftsbibliothek, MS 911, 44 and 226), which clearly match the modern German *taufe* and *Ostern*. If Udolph were correct that the Old High German *Ostarun* derives from the plural for 'baptisms' we might logically expect to find the word in its singular form for 'baptism', but instead we find the word *tauffi*. Furthermore, words deriving from the same root as *tauffi* (Proto-Germanic **daup-a*) have been used throughout the Germanic language group for the Christian act of baptism. These examples include the Old English *dyppan*, Old Saxon *dôpian* and Old High German *toufen*, all of which predate the appearance of *vatni ausa* in Old Norse texts. But perhaps more significantly, the word is also found as *daupjan* in the Gothic translation of the Bible by Bishop Wulfila dating to the fourth century AD (Streitberg 1919, 251; Corinthians I, 1:13–17), and is therefore the oldest recorded Germanic word for 'baptise'.

Alternatively, there may be a more direct route by which *Ostern* and *Ostermonat* could have entered the German language (Green 2000, 353; Sermon 2008, 337). Much of western Germany and the Low Countries were converted to Christianity by clerics from England, including St Willibrord (658–739 AD), St Boniface (baptised Winfrith, c. 673–754 AD), and St Willibald (c. 700–787 AD). These Anglo-Saxon missionaries spoke a very similar language (and dialects) to those they were seeking to convert, in particular the Frisians and continental Saxons. They were therefore likely to have been preaching in their native tongue on subjects like Easter, and perhaps celebrating the festival by its Old English name during the course of their missionary work. The Laws of King Ine (c. 694 AD) and King Alfred (c. 893 AD) strongly suggest that *Eastron* was used as the paschal festival name in Wessex, and given that Boniface had spent his early life in a monastery at Exeter, he can be assumed to have known the festival by its Old English name. In 722 AD Pope Gregory II consecrated Boniface as a regional bishop and instructed him to only baptise his German converts at Easter and Whitsun: 'However, the holy sacrament of baptism is not to be provided unless during the Paschal festival and Pentecost' *Sacrosancti autem baptismi sacramentum non nisi in paschali festivitate et pentecosten noverit esse praebendum* (Tangl 1916, 31–33: letter 18). In a subsequent letter (738 AD) Boniface asks the English to pray for the conversion of the continental Saxons saying 'we are of one and the same blood and bone' *De uno sanguine et de uno osse sumus* (Tangl 1916, 74–75: letter 46). Based on this evidence it is safe assume that Boniface did indeed preach to the Saxon converts in his/their native tongue (and not in Latin), and in doing so could have introduced *Eastron* as the name of the festival at which many of them were baptised.

Furthermore, during his missionary activities Boniface wrote back to England requesting copies of Bede's works: twice to Egbert archbishop of York and once to Hwaetbert abbot of Wearmouth (Tangl 1916, 156–159 and 206–207: letters 75, 76 and 91); as did his successor Lull in correspondence with Cuthbert abbot Wearmouth and Jarrow (Tangl 1916, 250–252 and 263–265, letters 116, 126 and 127), who in one letter apologises for the slow progress in the scriptorium due to the harsh winter of 763–764 AD. From these letters we know that Lull was sent copies of Bede's metrical and prose *Vita Sancti Cuthberti* (Lives of St Cuthbert) and *De Templo* (On the Temple). However, there is evidence that other works by Bede were sent to Germany from the Tyne and Wear monasteries, including the two earliest known examples of Bede's *De Temporum Ratione* (Wallis 1999, lxxxvi). The first consists of three fragments from a single codex written in Northumbrian uncial script of the mid-eighth century, which given their north German provenance may be linked to Boniface and the Anglo-Saxon missions (Bückeburg, Niedersachsiche Staatsarchiv, Depot 3, ff. i–viii; Münster in Westfalen, Staatsarchiv, MS I. 243, ff. 1–2 and ff. 11–12; Braunschweig, Stadtbibliothek, fragment 70). The second example is a fragment from different codex found at Darmstadt in southern Germany, and is again written in Northumbrian uncial, and possibly within Bede's lifetime (Darmstadt, Hessische Landes und Hochschulbibliothek, Hs 4262). Unfortunately, none of these fragments derives from the relevant chapter *De Mensibus Anglorum*; nevertheless, the provenance of the last fragment is particularly interesting given Darmstadt's close proximity to the historic city of Mainz (a distance of 24 miles or 39 kilometres). Boniface was appointed bishop of Mainz in 745 AD, and its first archbishop in 747 AD. He held this position until the year of his death, when Boniface appointed Lull (c. 710–786 AD) his successor in 754 AD. Therefore, in Lull we have a:

1. cleric from Wessex who was likely familiar with *Eastron* as the Old English festival name,

2. requesting the works of Bede from the abbot of Monkwearmouth and Jarrow,

3. which based on the Darmstadt fragment may have included *De Temporum Ratione*,

4. delivered to his archbishopric in Mainz where the spoken language was Old High German,

5. in the right time frame (from 754 to 786 AD) to influence the vernacular name *Ostarun*,

6. as seen in the *Abrogans* attributed Arbeo bishop of Freising (from 764 to 783 AD).

These earlier missionaries were later followed by Alcuin (c. 735–804 AD), a leading scholar and teacher in the court of Charlemagne. Alcuin was born in Northumbria and educated at York where he became well acquainted with the works of Bede. He met Charlemagne at Parma in 781 AD and was appointed master of the palace school in Aachen. Here Alcuin is known to have built up a considerable library, which is likely to have included Bede's *De Temporum Ratione* with its reference to *Eosturmonath*. It was under Alcuin that the Frankish historian Einhard (770–840 AD) was to study, and later write the *Vita Karoli Magni* with its reference to *Ostarmanoth*. So, in giving this 'new' name to the month of April Charlemagne could have been influenced both by his teacher Alcuin, and by Bede's influential work on time (Dutton, 1998, 32):

For his other disciplines, he took as his teacher Alcuin of Britain, also known as Albinus who was a deacon as well, but from the Saxon people. He was the most learned man in the entire world. [Charlemagne] invested a great deal of time and effort studying rhetoric, dialectic and particularly astronomy with him. He learned the art of calculation and with deep purpose and great curiosity investigated the movements of the stars. (*Vita Karoli Magni*, chapter 25)

While it has been suggested that the Carolingian (Frankish) name *Ostarmanoth* could have developed independently in Germany, as the month in which the Christian festival *Ostarun* most often occurred (Shaw 2011, 95-96), this does not explain how the festival name arose in Old High German. Based on the preceding evidence, it is possible that the eighth-century German converts and Frankish scholars simply adopted the Old English festival and month names (*Eastron* and *Eastermonath*) into their native language, which subsequently appeared in Old High German orthography as *Ostarun* and *Ostarmanoth*. The observed morphological changes would be explained in linguistic terms as resulting from a 'loan translation' or calque (word-for-word or root-for-root translation) of the Old English festival and month names' original semantic values (meanings); where the early German clerics recognised their 'east' and 'month' etymologies (word origins) and translated the respective name elements into Old High German (OE *east/eost* = OHG *ost* + OE *monath* = OHG *manoth*).

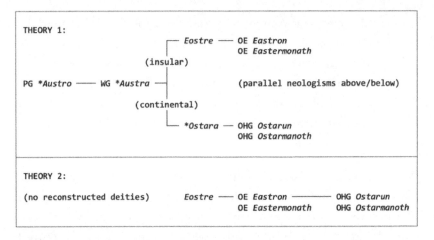

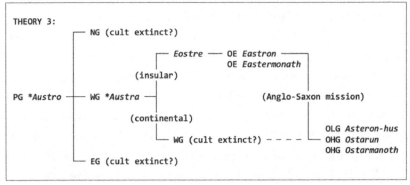

Table 13. Competing theories to explain the development of German festival and month names (PG = Proto-Germanic, NG = North Germanic, WG = West Germanic, EG = East Germanic, OE = Old English, OHG = Old High German, OLG = Old Low German or Old Saxon).

Having completed this overview we can now compare the two principal theories regarding the origin of the Old High German festival name *Ostarun* (see table 13): firstly, that supported by Jacob Grimm (1835) with its origin based on the reconstructed goddess name **Ostara* (theory 1), and secondly, that supported by Dennis Green (2000) with its origin based on the Old English festival name *Eastron* (theory 2). While both theories are logical and consistent, the strength of the second theory is that it relies solely on the available (observed) evidence, with no requirement for any reconstructed deities or parallel neologisms (changes in meaning: from pagan goddess name to Christian festival name). That being said, the suggestion that the Old English festival and month names were loaned into Old High German, in the context of the Anglo-Saxon mission, does not preclude the existence of an earlier Proto-Germanic goddess cult, or discount Bede's claim that the goddess *Eostre* was worshipped in early Anglo-Saxon England (see table 13, theory 3). If we accept the premiss that a Proto-Germanic and subsequent West Germanic goddess cult (**Austro* > **Austra*) may provide the origin for Bede's goddess *Eostre*, then at some point in time this cult must have become extinct in the North Germanic and East Germanic branches of the Germanic language group. Hence, it is conceivable that the goddess cult also became extinct in the continental West Germanic branch (on the European mainland), but survived longer in the insular West Germanic branch (on the island of Britain): where the goddess name was adopted as the Old English name for the Christian Paschal festival and then reintroduced to Germany during the Anglo-Saxon mission. I favour this latter theory because it: (a) provides a simple explanation for close parallel between the Old English and Old High German festival and month names, and (b) does not preclude existence of an ancestral Proto-Germanic or earlier Indo-European goddess cult, which will be discussed in the next chapter. Nevertheless, I acknowledge that this long-standing debate is far from over.

CHAPTER 5

Ushas, *Eos* and Aurora:
The Dawn of Indo-European Mythology

During the late sixteenth century European travellers and linguists began to notice similarities between their own languages and those of Persia (Iran) and the Indian sub-continent, with some positing their development from a shared ancestral language (Mallory and Adams 2006, 1–11). However, it was not until the late eighteenth century that the idea was fully articulated and began to take hold, when in 1786 Sir William Jones then president of the Asiatic Society of Bengal gave a lecture 'on the Hindus' in which he noted the striking similarities between Sanskrit, Greek and Latin, which along with Gothic, Celtic and Persian, suggested they had 'sprung from some common source':

> The Sanscrit [*sic*] language, whatever be its antiquity, is of a wonderful structure; more perfect than the Greek, more copious than the Latin, and more exquisitely refined than either, yet bearing to both of them a stronger affinity, both in the roots of verbs and in the forms of grammar, than could possibly have been produced by accident; so strong indeed, that no philologer could examine them all three, without believing them to have sprung from some common source, which, perhaps, no longer exists: there is a similar reason, though not quite so forcible, for

supposing that both the Gothick [*sic*] and the Celtick [*sic*], though blended with a very different idiom, had the same origin with the Sanscrit [*sic*]; and the old Persian might be added to the same family, if this were the place for discussing any question concerning the antiquities of Persia. (Shore 1807, 3: 34–35)

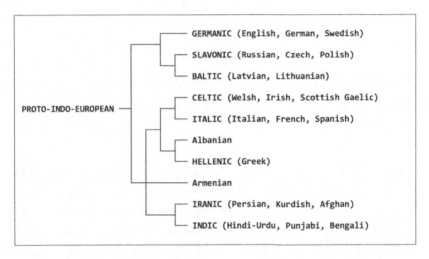

Table 14. Suggested relationships between the principal branches of the Indo-European language family (upper case) with examples of their modern languages (standard case).

In this important statement Jones identified a clear relationship between the Indic (Sanskrit), Hellenic (Greek), Italic (Latin) Germanic (Gothic), Celtic and Iranic (Old Persian) branches of an extensive unnamed family of languages (see table 14), to which the Baltic and Slavonic branches would later be added (Mallory and Adams 2006, 12–38). These languages would come to be known as Indo-European, and in Germany as *Indogermanisch* (Indo-Germanic) due to the historic spread of the language family: from India in the south-east to Iceland in the north-west. The relationship with Sanskrit was also recognised by Jacob Grimm (1848) in his *Ge-*

schichte der deutschen Sprache (History of the German Language). Over the next two centuries archaeologists and linguists would attempt to identify the homeland and material culture of the first Proto-Indo-European speakers (Renfrew 1987), and to reconstruct their ancient language through comparative linguistics, by examining the changes within and between its descendant languages (Mallory and Adams 2006, 39–50). In a parallel process known as 'comparative mythology' these early researchers also attempted to reconstruct the Proto-Indo-European gods and goddesses, assuming a similar evolutionary development from a common body of ancestral mythology (Mallory and Adams 2006, 423–441). This ancient cosmology was believed to have comprised a number of elemental deities including the Sun, the Moon, the Sky and the Dawn. One of its leading proponents was Friedrich Max Müller (1823–1900) who in 1856 suggested that a solar mythology could be observed in core narratives of the oldest Hindu (Vedic) religious texts, which he believed were closest to an original Proto-Indo-European mythology (Müller 1909).

Though such ideas are now much criticised and subject to academic deconstruction, being viewed by some as pseudo-mythology, it is nevertheless worth considering the known dawn deities recorded in various Indo-European speaking cultures. The earliest of these appears in the ancient Sanskrit hymns of the *Rigveda* (book 1, hymns 48–49, 92, 113, 123–124; book 3, hymn 61; book 4, hymns 51–52; book 5, hymns 79–80; book 6, hymns 64–65; book 7, hymns 75–81; book 10, hymn 172). These hymns or *sukta* are the foundation texts of the Hindu religion and are thought to have been composed first orally in the mid to late second millennium BC, and then codified at the end of that period. In these ancient chants we find the Hindu goddess of the dawn *Usha* or *Ushas* (उषस्) being carried aloft in a shining car pulled by red cows, arising each morning in the east to announce the arrival of the sun god *Surya* (book 5, hymn 80):

The singers welcome with their hymns and praises the Goddess Dawn [*Devim Ushasam*] who bringeth in the sunlight, Sublime, by Law true to eternal Order, bright on her path, red-tinted, far-refulgent. She comes in front, fair, rousing up the people, making the pathways easy to be travelled. High, on her lofty chariot, all-impelling, Dawn gives her splendour at the days' beginning. She, harnessing her car with purple [ruddy] oxen, injuring none, hath brought perpetual riches. Opening paths to happiness, the Goddess shines, praised by all, giver of every blessing. With changing tints she gleams in double splendour while from the eastward she displays her body. She travels perfectly the path of Order, nor fails to reach, as one who knows, the quarters. As conscious that her limbs are bright with bathing, she stands, as 'twere, erect that we may see her. Driving away malignity and darkness, Dawn [*Usha*], Child of Heaven, hath come to us with lustre. The Daughter of the Sky, like some chaste woman, bends, opposite to men, her forehead downward. The Maid, disclosing boons to him who worships, hath brought again the daylight as aforetime. (Griffith 1896, 1: 547–548)

In subsequent depictions we find *Surya* riding his horse drawn chariot flanked by *Usha* (dawn) and *Pratyusha* (twilight), both armed with bows and arrows to banish the darkness of the night. One of the earliest such depictions is a carved stone relief at the temple of Bodh Gaya and is thought to date from the second to first century BC (Mitra 1878, plate 50). Later examples of this same scene include a tenth-century black basalt sculpture from Patna, a thirteenth-century limestone sculpture from Hassan (V&A Museum, London, accession numbers IM.109-1916 and IS.76-1965), a fourteenth-century painted fabric *mandala* from Kathmandu (Metropolitan Museum, New York, accession number 2012.462), and a similar sixteenth-century *mandala* also from Nepal (Walters Museum, Baltimore, accession number F.195). The distribution of these examples (apart from Hassan) mirrors the present-day regions where the ancient Vedic goddess is still worshipped: in the Indian states of Bihar and eastern Uttar Pradesh, and in the adjacent Madhesh province of Nepal. During the festival of *Chhath Puja* the sun god *Surya* and his wife *Usha* (or *Chhathi Maiya*) are honoured, and thanked for the gifts of life they bestow upon the earth. The festival celebrated twice a year at *Chaiti Chhath* (in March or April) and *Kartik Chhath* (in October or November) with dawn offerings (*Usha Arghya*) made on its fourth and final day. The same Vedic dawn goddess is also honoured by the Zoroastrian community in Iran, and the Parsis (as they are known) in India. Though a minority group in today's Iran, the Zoroastrians are a living monument to Persia's ancient (pre-Islamic) religion and culture. Their book of common prayer the *Khorda Avesta* contains a prayer (*gah* or *geh*) for each phase of the day, with the goddess *Ushah* praised in the midnight to dawn prayer *Ushahin Gah* (Geldner 1896, 2, 58–59; *Gah* 5.5):

> We worship the beautiful *Ushah*; we worship the radiant *Ushah*, with swift horses... the swift *Ushah*, with swift horses, which appear throughout the seven regions of the earth; we worship that *Ushah*. (Darmesteter 1898, 3, 216)

In southern Europe (and the Mediterranean) we find similar dawn deities with cognate names in ancient Greek and Roman mythology. The Greek goddess *Eos* (Ἠώς > Ἕως) who arose on her chariot each morning in the east to announce the arrival of her brother the sun god *Helios* (Ἥλιος), is mirrored by her Roman equivalent *Aurora* and brother *Sol*. Early descriptions of the goddess *Eos* are found in the eighth-century BC epic poems attributed to Homer, the *Iliad* (Murray 1925, 336–337 and 620–623) and the *Odyssey* (Murray 1919, 2: 8–9 and 390–391), and as the principal subject for one of the 87 *Orphic Hymns* (Athanassakis and Wolkow 2013, 61–62):

> Now Dawn [*Eos*] the saffron-robed arose from the streams of Oceanus to bring light to immortals and to mortal men... But soon as early Dawn [*Eos*] appeared, the rosy-fingered, then

gathered the folk about the pyre of glorious Hector. (*Iliad* 19.1–2 and 24.788–789)

Now when that brightest of stars rose which ever comes to herald the light of early Dawn [*Eos*]... And now would the rosy-fingered Dawn [*Eos*] have arisen... the golden-throned Dawn [*Eos*] at the streams of Oceanus... her swift-footed horses that bring light to men, Lampus and Phaethon, who are the colts that bear the Dawn [*Eos*]. (*Odyssey* 13.93–94 and 23.241–246)

Hear, O goddess, you bring the light of day to mortals, re-splendent Dawn [*Eos*], you blush throughout the world, messen-ger of the great, the illustrious Titan. Murky, dark, journeying night you send below the earth when you arrive; mortal men you lead to work as you tend to their lives. The race of mortal men delights in you, no one escapes your sight as you look down from on high, when from your eyelids you shake off sweet sleep, when there is joy for every mortal, for every reptile, for animals, for birds, for the broods the sea contains. All blessings that come from work are your gift. Goddess, blessed and pure, give more sacred light to the initiates. (*Orphic Hymns* 78.1–14)

Later descriptions of the Roman goddess *Aurora* are found in the first-century BC poems of Ovid and Virgil, the *Heroides* (Show-erman 1914, 211–213) and the *Aeneid* (Fairclough 1916, 434–435), in which the authors are clearly equating *Aurora* with *Eos* whose Trojan lover was Tithonus (Murray 1919, 1: 170–171):

A Phrygian was Aurora's mate; yet he was carried away by the goddess who sets the last bound to the advance of night. (*Heri-odes* 16.201–202)

And now early Dawn [Aurora], leaving the saffron bed of Titho-nus, was sprinkling her fresh rays upon the earth. (*Aeneid* 4.584–585)

Figure 2. Late fourth-century BC terracotta dish from Apuia in Italy depicting the arrival of Eos in her horse drawn chariot.

> Now Dawn [*Eos*] arose from her couch from beside lordly Ti-
> thonus, to bear light to the immortals and to mortal men.
> (*Odyssey* 5.1–2)

A significant number of ancient Greek ceramics that are decorated
with mythological scenes are thought to contain depictions of the
goddess *Eos*, with some identifications more obvious than others.
A particularly good example is a late fourth-century BC terracotta
lekanis (dish) from Apuia in southern Italy (see figure 2), which
depicts *Eos*, with a radiant halo, in her chariot (*quadriga*) dawn by
four white horses (Metropolitan Museum, New York, accession
number 1969.11.8). A clearly related image of *Aurora* in her chariot, chasing away the moon goddess *Luna*, is depicted on the
breastplate of Prima Porta statue of the Emperor Augustus, which
dates to early first century AD (Vatican Museums, Rome, accession number 2290).

Further away in northern Europe we find evidence of an isolated dawn goddess in the mythology of the Baltic-speaking
peoples, who were among last European nations to be converted
to Christianity following the Northern Crusades of the twelfth to
fourteenth centuries. In 1615 the Polish historian and theologian
Jan Łasicki's work 'On the Gods of the Samogitians' was published
in Basel, which lists over seventy pagan deities, including a description of the Samogitian (Lithuanian) dawn goddess: *Ausca, dea
est radiorum solis vel occumbentis, vel supra horizontem ascendentis*
'Ausca is the goddess of the rays of the sun, either setting or rising
above the horizon' (Łasicki 1615, 47). The existence of such a cult
would appear to be supported by later Baltic folklore, where we
find related deity names and personifications of natural phenomena: Lithuanian *aušra* (dawn) and *aušrinė* (morning star); Latvian
ausma (dawn), *austrumi* (east) and *auseklis* (morning star). The
basic premise of Proto-Indo-European mythology is that: (a)
where comparative linguistics suggests the deity names (under
consideration) share a common Proto-Indo-European root, and

64

(b) where comparative mythology reveals similar deity traits and characteristics, then (c) the deities are likely to have developed from the same ancestral Proto-Indo-European cult. Recognition that the Sanskrit *Ushas*, Farsi *Ushah*, Greek *Eos* and Latin *Auroa* appear to meet these criteria—deriving from the same linguistic root and sharing similar chariot-riding, sun-heralding, east-rising, and rose or saffron-coloured dawn goddess characteristics—ensured their early admission into the reconstructed Proto-Indo-European pantheon. And for those who accepted Jan Łasicki's sixteenth-century testimony, the Samogitian *Ausca* was also admitted into this fold. These ideas would subsequently lead German linguists and folklorists to suggest that *Eostre* and/or *Ostara* was the Germanic reflex of the same dawn goddess (Helm 1950, 9). Current research reconstructs the ancestral goddess name and word for the 'dawn' as *$h_a\acute{e}us\bar{o}s$*, formed from the verbal root *h_aewes-* 'shine' that is also thought to underlie words for the 'east' *$h_aeust(e)ro$-* and 'gold' *h_ae-usom* (Mallory and Adams 2006, 300–301, 409, 432 and 486).

Recent criticism of Proto-Indo-European studies and mythology (influenced by wider trends within cultural studies) has tended to focus on what are deemed to be: (a) the 'simplistic' and 'idealised' (though not intrinsically flawed) models applied by earlier researchers, (b) the perceived political and cultural biases of earlier researchers (while often ignoring the critic's own contemporary biases), and (c) characterising their hypothetical (but not necessarily false) deities as 'pseudo-mythology'. In regard to the dawn goddesses discussed in this chapter, doubts have been raised about the veracity of Jan Łasicki's (1615) list of Samogitian deities, and the degree to which modern nationalism may have influenced the reconstruction of Baltic folklore and mythology. During the Latvian and Lithuanian period of national awakening, starting in the mid-nineteenth century, and their twentieth-century struggles for independence (from Germany, Russia and the Soviet Union), the folklore and mythology of these Baltic-speaking nations has played a central role in the development of their national identities and political consciousness. It is therefore no coincidence that the first Lithuanian national newspaper printed from 1883 to 1886 was named *Auszra* (Dawn), a title with both cultural and political symbolism. While these influences clearly need to be understood, the evidence for a Baltic dawn goddess cannot be completely discounted. Similar criticisms have also been levelled against Jacob Grimm's reconstructed goddesses *Hruoda*, *Ostara*, and *Zisa*, which cannot be historically attested (Grimm 1835, 180-189). The influence of German nationalism on mythology and folklore will be considered in chapter 7. Nevertheless, if we accept the possibility that comparative linguistics (of etymologically related deity names), combined with comparative mythology (of their recorded traits and characteristics), can indicate descent from a shared ancestral mythology—as is almost certainly the case for the Semitic language group and its ancient pantheon—then it is not unreasonable to look for other possible examples within the cultures of related-language speakers. While we should be aware of (and transparent about) possible historical biases and influences on the mythological and folkloric evidence (whether social, political or religious), we should not shy away from continuing research in this area.

A West Slavic conundrum

West Slavic	Language	Easter Name
Polabian	Draveno-Polabian (extinct)	Jostrâi
Polonian	Old Polish (dialect)	Jastry
Pomeranian	Kashubian	Jastrë
Pomeranian	Slovincian (extinct)	Jastra
Lusatian	Upper Sorbian	Jutry
Lusatian	Lower Sorbian	Jatšy

Table 15. Easter names occurring in some (northern) West Slavic languages and dialects.

In parts of eastern Germany, and some of its former territories now in Poland, a number of West Slavic languages and dialects share related Easter names that are not found in any of the other Slavic languages (see table 15). Like *Ostern* theses names exists in their plural forms, and, given their Kashubian and Polabian spellings (*Jastrë* and *Jostråi*), many researchers have concluded they are simply loan words from Old High German, resulting from the medieval conquest and conversion of the western Slavs, and later colonisation by German-speaking settlers (Bielfeldt 1977, 452). This argument is borne out by German dialect names recorded (before 1945) in these same former German territories: *Ostere* or *Ostre* in northern Pomerania and East Prussia, and *Ostera* or *Ostra* in southern Pomerania (König 1979, 188-189). However, an alternative theory (Krogmann 1937) points out that these West Slavic names, and the Upper Sorbian name (*Jutry*) in particular, share a similar morphology to nouns and adverbs found throughout the Slavic language group meaning 'morning' or 'daybreak' (*jutro* and *utro*), 'in the morning' (*jutre* and *utre*) and 'tomorrow' (*zautra*). These examples are all found in Old Church Slavonic, the first Slavic literary language dating back to the ninth century AD, with an interesting occurrence of *zaustra* in the eleventh century *Psalterium Sinaiticum* (Lunt 2001, 221). The last example can be equated with the Bulgarian and Macedonian dialect word *zastra* (tomorrow), and more distantly with the Old Polish words *justrzenka* (dawn light), *justrz-ejszy* (of tomorrow) and *naza-justrz* (to the following day). These words could indicate that the Proto-Slavic root originally contained a medial /s/, which was lost in almost all the later Slavic languages, but survived in a few dialect forms (Dolgopolsky 2008, 192–193). While the presence of this medial /s/ is disputed by some, it does provide an alternative (yet still distantly related) etymology for these unusual West Slavic Easter names. That being said, the close and long-standing contacts between the Slavic and Germanic-speaking peoples are known to have resulted in numerous Germanic loanwords within the Slavic languages (Pronk-Tiethoff 2013, 69), which therefore seems to provide the most likely explanation. While it may appear more complex to suppose one loan (from Old English to Old High German) followed by a loan of that loan (from Middle High German to West Slavic), it is possible to identify even longer sequences of borrowings:

> Hebrew *Pesach* > Aramaic *Pascha* > Greek *Pascha* > Latin *Pascha* > Old Galician-Portuguese *Pascua* > Sinhalese *Pasku*

Sri Lanka (formerly known as Ceylon) was subject to Portuguese missionary activity from the early sixteenth to the mid-seventeenth century, which established a Sinhalese-speaking Christian minority on the largely Buddhist island, and resulted in the Old Portuguese festival name (*Pascua*) being borrowed into the insular Indic language (Sinhalese *Pasku*). Whereas in the rest of the Indian subcontinent, which was more heavily influenced by British missionary activity, versions of the the English festival name Easter were borrowed into the various Indic and Dravidian languages (as *Istar* and *Istara*). The relevance of these examples is that: (a) the number of preceding borrowings of the festival name appears to be largely immaterial, and (b) it is the vernacular festival name used by the foreign missionaries that is borrowed into the converts' native language.

CHAPTER 6

Eggs, Rabbits and Hares:
Christian Symbols or Cultural Appropriation?

The two Easter symbols that are most often said to be associated with the goddess *Eostre* (and her Germanic reconstruction *Ostara*) are the Easter egg and the Easter rabbit or hare (German *Ostereier* and *Osterhase*). The goddess' supposed connection with eggs can be traced back to Jacob Grimm, who argued that *Ostereier* and their use in popular games were vestiges of the cult of *Ostara* that the church had been forced to tolerate (Grimm 1883, 2, 780). Her supposed connection with the hare can be traced back to the German philologist Adolf Holtzmann, who believed that the *Osterhase* most likely represented the beast of *Ostara* (Holtzman 1874, 141). But is there any factual basis for these often-repeated claims?

The egg is perhaps the most well-known symbol of Easter, and there is much conjecture about its adoption by the Church, with many references pointing to possible pre-Christian pagan origins. Eggs are known to be very ancient religious symbols, appearing in virtually all the world's faiths, both today and in antiquity (Newall 1971). In many of these contexts eggs can be seen to operate as symbols of rebirth and new life, especially in the spring when birds begin to nest and domesticated fowl start to produce more eggs (with the increasing hours of daylight). Eggs are a required food within the Jewish *Seder* or Passover meal, at this same time of year, and make perfect sense as a Christian metaphor for the resurrection of Jesus. The Paschal egg (Greek Πασχαλινό αυγό) tradition first appears within the Christian communities of the Eastern Orthodox and Eastern Catholic churches. An often quoted (yet relatively late) reference by the English linguist Thomas Hyde (1636–1703) suggests that this may have been among the early Christians of Mesopotamia:

> *Is apud Mesopotamienses Christianos exerceri solet a tempore Paschatis... Hoc enim tempore Chrisianorum pueri emunt sibi quotquot possunt Ova, Quae etiam rubro colore inficiunt, in memorium effusi sanguinis Salvatoris eo tempore crucifixi.* (Hyde 1694, 237)

> Among the Mesopotamian Christians there is a custom practised at Easter time... when their children buy as many eggs as they can, which they stain with a red colour, in memory of the blood shed by our Saviour who was crucified at this time [of year]. (author's translation)

This 'red egg' tradition was highlighted by Venetia Newall in her influential folklore study *An Egg at Easter*, in which she described how the Chaldean and Syrian Christians still maintain the same egg dying tradition (Newall 1971, 207–231). While its exact point of origin remains uncertain, the tradition clearly spread throughout the eastern churches of the Byzantine empire, centred on Constantinople (modern Istanbul), and across the nations of central and eastern Europe that were converted to Christianity by its Eastern Orthodox saints. This explains the prevalence of egg decorating traditions among the Slavic-speaking peoples, who have developed highly decorated and variously coloured forms. In the Greek Orthodox church eggs are still dyed red in memory of the blood shed by Christ, then blessed by the local priest on Holy Saturday, and given as symbolic gifts on Easter Sunday accompanied by Greek phrase *Christos Anesti* (Χριστός Ανέστη) 'Christ is Risen!'

The symbolism of the Paschal egg appears rather later in western Europe and is often said to have arrived in England during the late thirteenth century (Newall 1971, 219 and 263; Hutton 1996, 198). There are two principal sources for this often-repeated claim. The first can be found in the Household Roll of Eleanor de Montfort, Countess of Leicester, in 1265 (British Library, Additional MS 8877) when her family and household were spending Easter at Odiham Castle in Hampshire (Botfield 1841, 16-17). Here she is recorded as having received a large quantity of eggs costing four shillings one pence ha'penny *(Die Paschae, pro Comitissa et praedictis... Ova, iiijs id ob)*, which the nineteenth-century editor elaborates upon is his introduction:

> Eggs seem to have been an important item in the culinary processes of the thirteenth century. The price of them varied from 3½d to 4½d per hundred... On Easter Sunday upwards of twelve hundred were purchased; of which the greater part were, probably, stained and given away as Pasque eggs. (Botfield 1841, xlvi)

The second source can be found in the financial accounts of Edward I, when in 1290 the king and his household were spending Easter at his manor of Isenhampstead (Chenies) in Buckinghamshire. These accounts record that on Easter Sunday (*Dominica in festo paschae*) the kitchen and scullery received numerous supplies for the Easter feast, including four hundred and fifty eggs at a cost of eighteen pence *(p. iiij C di. ov. xviij d)*. In a footnote to this entry the nineteenth-century editor likewise surmises:

> Part of these four hundred and a half of eggs might have been purchase for the purpose of being stained with various colours, and given as Easter presents to the royal household, a custom which generally prevailed in Catholic times in token of the resurrection, and still continues in the Greek church. In some parts of the north of England such eggs are still also presented to children at Easter, and called paste (*pasque*) eggs. (Lysons 1806, 358–359)

71

However, as a forbidden food during the forty-day fast of *Quadragesima* or Lent (from the Old English *Lencten* for Spring), there would have been a glut of eggs at this time of year. It is worth noting that in Eleanor de Montfort's accounts for the week following Easter Sunday (Botfield 1841, 19), the same value of eggs were again purchased on both the Wednesday and Thursday—for four shillings one pence ha'penny (49.5 pence)—and on the Saturday for a staggering ten shillings nine pence ha'penny (129.5 pence). If these figures are resolved into multiples of exactly one hundred eggs, they reveal the huge quantity and depreciating value of eggs purchase during that week:

> Easter Sunday, 5th of April 1265, 49.5 pence (at 4.5 pence per 100 eggs) = 1100
>
> Wednesday 8th of April 1265, 49.5 pence (at 4.5 pence per 100 eggs) = 1100
>
> Thursday 9th of April 1265, 49.5 pence (at 4.5 pence per 100 eggs) = 1100
>
> Saturday 11th of April 1265, 129.5 pence (at 3.5 pence per 100 eggs) = 3700

While some of these eggs could have been gifted as Paschal eggs, this explanation is by no means certain. Other explanations have been offered, including: the countess's household being significantly larger than usual, that some medieval recipes required great numbers of eggs, and that these eggs may have been small in size due to the hen's poor diet (Labarge 1965, 82). Nevertheless, by the end of the Middle Ages it was becoming customary across much of western Europe to give eggs as symbolic gifts on Easter Sunday, when they could finally be eaten after the long Lenten fast (Italian *uova di Pasqua*, Spanish *huevos de Pascua*, French *Oeufs de Pâques*). However, the practice was not formally recognised by the Church of Rome until the early seventeenth century, when a Paschal egg blessing appeared in the first printing of the *Rituale Romanum*:

Benedictio ovorum: Subveniat, quaesumus Domine, tuae benedic-
tionis gratia huic ovorum creaturae, ut cibus salubris fiat fidelibus
tuis, in tuarum gratiarum actione sumentibus, ob resurrectionem
Domini nostri Jesu Christi. (Pope Paul V 1617, 255)

Blessing of eggs: Help us Lord, we ask you, that with the grace of your blessing on these living eggs, they become wholesome food for the faithful, received in thankfulness, for the resurrection of our Lord Jesus Christ. (author's translation)

One of the earliest references to 'Easter eggs' occurs in John Knox's *Historie of the Reformation of the Church of Scotland*, in which he describes an incident in 1565 when a Catholic priest in Edinburgh was punished for saying mass: 'Himself fast tyed to the said Crosse [Mercat Cross], where he tarried the space of one hour; During which time, the boyes served him with his Easter egges' (Knox 1644, 5: 404). Although describing events in sixteenth-century Scotland, this work was published almost a century later in London, and written in the standard (southern) English of that time. In the north of England and Lowland Scotland these eggs were generally known as 'Pace' or 'Paste' eggs, a name which is again derived from the Latin *Pascha* (via Norman French *Pasche* and Middle English *Paske > Pase*). However, it was not until the late nineteenth century that the 'Easter egg' was to become as widely popular in southern England (see the above quote from 1806), which coincided with the emergence of printed Easter cards, decorated paper-mache eggs (sometime filled with sweets or candy), and the chocolate eggs that we know today.

The Easter rabbit or hare (German *Osterhase*) appears much later in time and seems to have begun as a localised tradition in south-west Germany, where it was widely believed that hares laid eggs rather than giving birth to live-born young—possibly due to the similarity between a brown hare's (*Lepus europaeus*) scrape or form and a lapwing's (*Vanellus vanellus*) nest, which both occur on grassland in the spring (Nicholls 1993). The earliest known reference to these 'hare's eggs' is in a short phrase or saying (first published in 1574) by the German satirist Johann Fischart of Strasbourg:

> *Sorg nicht das dir der Haß vom Spieß entlauff:*
> *Haben wir nit die Eier, so braten wir das Nest.* (Fischart 1598, 140)

> Do not worry if the Hare escapes you;
> Should we miss his eggs, then we shall cook the nest. (Newell 1971, 324)

Nevertheless, the first specific reference to the *Osterhase* is provided by Georg Franck von Franckenau, a professor of medicine at the University of Heidelberg, in an essay published in 1682 under the Latin title *De Ovis Paschalibus* (On Easter Eggs):

> *In Germania Superiore, Palatinatu nostrate, Alsatia & vicinis locis,*
> *ut & in Westphalia vocantur hæc ova di Hasen-Eier a fabula, qua*
> *simplicioribus & infantibus imponunt Leporem (der Oster-Hase)*
> *ejusmodi ova excludere, & in hortis in gramine, fruticetis &c. ab-*
> *scondere ut studiosius a pueris investigentur, cum risu & jucunditate*
> *seniorum.* (Von Franckenau 1682: 6)

> In Upper Germany, our Palatinate, Alsace and neighbouring areas, and also in Westphalia, these eggs are called the Hare's-Eggs, a story, which the simple and childlike are told, that the hare (the Easter-Hare) lays eggs and hides them in gardens, in the grass and bushes etc., so the children eagerly search for them, to the smiles and delight of their elders. (author's translation)

While this tradition would seem to have arisen some three to four hundred years ago in south-west Germany and Alsace (now in France), it remained unknown in other parts of the country until the eighteenth century. Hares would have been a common sight in the fields at Easter, and thus provided a convenient ruse to explain the origin of the eggs purposely hidden in gardens for children to find. During the nineteenth century the influence of Easter cards and gifts was to make the Easter hare or rabbit popular throughout Europe. German immigrants then exported the custom to Britain and America where it evolved into the Easter Bunny (Winick 2016). Unlike the Easter egg, the Easter hare/rabbit has never been viewed as a Christian religious symbol, and has always been restricted to the more secular games and imagery associated with the holiday.

In short, there is no evidence to connect either eggs, rabbits or hares with Bede's goddess *Eostre*, or her Germanic reconstruction *Ostara*. The Christian symbolism associated with the Easter egg, or perhaps more correctly the Paschal egg, is first known to have arisen among the Christian communities of the eastern church—for whom the pagan Anglo-Saxons, and their goddess *Eostre*, would have been extremely remote. Following the Anglo-Saxons' conversion to Christianity (in the late sixth to seventh centuries AD) there is no evidence of the Paschal egg tradition in early medieval England. Furthermore, there is no evidence to suggest any continuity of symbols, customs or rituals between the pre-conversion and post-conversion festivals, and 'the modern observance of Easter owes nothing to Anglo-Saxon paganism, with the sole exception of its English name' (Parker 2022, 126). The first record of the Easter rabbit or *Osterhase* appears over a thousand years later in south-west Germany, and is largely unknown in England until the late nineteenth century. As such there is no evidence to suggest that Christians appropriated either: (a) the religious symbolism of the Paschal egg, or (b) the secular imagery of Easter rabbit, from any early Anglo-Saxon or ancient Germanic pagan practices.

CHAPTER II

CHAPTER 7

Osterberg and *Osterfeuer*:
Ostara and the Rise of German Nationalism

During the medieval period, when the European seats of learning were its great Christian monasteries, the classical sources and collected knowledge of the ancient world were copied in its scriptoria and studied in its many libraries. However, the more revered works were those thought to aid or shine light upon 'God's divine purpose' as revealed to them in the Bible, and through the teachings and doctrines of the church. With the onset of the European Renaissance (from the fifteenth to seventeenth century) and subsequent Enlightenment (from the seventeenth to eighteenth century) this interest in ancient learning, and Graeco-Roman culture in particular, became less constrained by Christian theology, which led to great advances in artistic, literary and scientific enquiry. These changes coincided with the development and spread of the movable-type printing press (by Johannes Gutenberg in 1440), which led to an explosion of books, maps, illustrations and pamphlets on a diverse and ever-growing range of subjects. During this period we begin to see a growing interest in not only the antiquities and mythology of Mediterranean world, but also in the ancient monuments, languages and cultures of northern Europe, as seen in Sebastian Münster's *Cosmographia* (1550). This and subsequent books sought to explain the origins of the various peoples and nations of Europe, often focussing on their ancient religious beliefs—a trend that we have already seen in works by German authors, including Philipp Clüver's *Germaniae Antiquae* (1616), Johannes Schild's *De Caucis, Nobilissimo Veteris Germaniae Populo* (1649), and Johann Vorburg's *Historia Romano-Germanica* (1659). Long before the work of Jacob Grimm (1835), numerous German place names containing the initial elements *oster-* or *osten-* were said to have been related to the worship of the goddess Ostara. These included the many *Osterberg* mountain and hill names associated with the German Easter bonfire tradition, along with sites in ancient forest and woodland locations. An early example of this is provided by Ernst Wasserbach (1664–1709) the mayor of Barntrup and later Blomberg:

> *Hic Teutonicimontes, Lucos ac nemora consecrata Diis apud Kolstede et fanum Osterae Deae prope Osterholtz.* (Wasserbach 1698, 7)

> Here in the Teutoburg, the forests and groves were consecrated to the Gods at Kohlstädt, and a sanctuary of the goddess *Ostera* near Oesterholz. (author's translation)

Similar interpretations were offered by Luneberg Mushard (1672–1708), the rector of the cathedral school at Bremen, in relation to place names in Lower Saxony. In his *De Ostera Saxonum* (concerning *Ostera* of the Saxons) he suggests that the names of sacred forest and groves once dedicated to the goddess still survive at Osterwede, Osterhagen and Osterndorf, with an important temple site (*Templum Osterae*) at Osterholz (Mushard 1702, 10). These ideas appear to have influenced Ernst Rathlef, who similarly argued that the Saxon goddess *Eostra* had been worshipped with great fire ceremonies on the Osterberg uplands near Nienburg in Lower Saxony (Rathlef 1766, 5–44).

Figure 3. Arminius Monument (Hermannsdenkmal) constructed in the Teutoburg forest near Detmold in 1875.

With the advent the Romantic Movement and rise of ethnic or Romantic Nationalism, beginning in the late eighteenth to early nineteenth century, European politics, history and the arts would converge on more emotional expressions and ideas around identity and nationhood. Language was a central and determining feature of the various nationalist movements, which included Celtic, Germanic, Baltic and Slavic nationalism, and were often seen as great 'revivals' or 'awakenings' of collective national consciousness. The German Romantic poet and philosopher Johann Gottfried von Herder (1744–1803) believed that the spirit of the German nation (*Deutscher Volksgeist*) was to be found in the folk songs, dances and traditions of the ordinary people. At the start of this period Germany consisted of numerous semi-independent German-speaking territories and states, but, with an ever growing tide of linguistic and cultural nationalism, it would culminate in the unification of Germany in 1871. This period saw a yearning for a past Germanic golden age to rival that of ancient Greece and Rome, and there is perhaps no greater expression of this than the massive *Hermannsdenkmal* erected near Detmold between 1838 and 1875 (see figure 3). This 50-metre high copper statue and stone pedestal celebrated the national hero Arminius (*Hermann*) and his Germanic tribes, who in 9 AD inflicted a catastrophic defeat on the Roman general Varus and his three legions in the Teutoburg forest (Sharma 1995, 75–120). In this same heroic and mythical landscape other monuments were constructed (at Enger and Herford) to the pagan Saxon king Widukind who resisted Charlemagne and the Holy Roman Empire; while at the nearby Externsteine rock formation connections were made with the *Irminsul* or sacred great pillar of the Saxons. This was fertile ground for what came to be known as the *Völkisch* movement with its leanings towards the occult, which saw the appearance of many dubious (and often clearly fabricated) historical, mythological and folkloric sources. One such example is an Old Saxon charm or remedy for unproductive land, said to have been found in a manuscript at Corvey Abbey (Kloster Korvei) but subsequently lost (Hocker 1853, 224;

Montanus 1858, 28):

Eostar Eostar	Ostar Ostar
eordhan modor	Erdenmutter,
geune these	Lasse diesen
acera veaxendra	Acker wachsen,
and virdhendra	Laß ihn grünen,
eacniendra	Laß ihn blühen,
eluiendra	Fruchte tragen,
fridha him!	Gieb ihm Frieden!
that his yrdh si gefridhod	Daß die Erde sei gefriedet,
and heo si geborgun	Daß sie sei geborgen,
as his halige	Wie die heiligen,
the on heofenum sint.	Die im himmel sind.

The first two lines of the charm were published by Nikolaus Hocker in 1853, with the full text (and German translation) published five years later by Vincenz Jacob von Zuccalmaglio under the pen name Montanus. The text implores *Eostar* the earth's mother to grant you fields that are growing, thriving and productive, and to free you (from what ails your land), so that the earth is protected and made safe like the saints in heaven. The problem with this text, in addition to the original manuscript being missing, is that that it could all be derived from a much longer Old English field remedy known as the *Æcerbot* (British Library, MS Cotton Caligula A. VII, ff.177r–178r), which dates to the late tenth or early eleventh century and is attached to a copy of the Old Saxon gospel poem the *Heliand*. The corresponding lines from the *Æcerbot* manuscript (omitting the text in square brackets) provide a very close match to the Corvey Abbey charm:

51: Erce, Erce, Erce, eorþan modor,

52: geunne þe se [alwalda, ece drihten],

53: æcera wexendra and wridendra,

54: eacniendra [and] elniendra,

59: [Geunne] him [ece drihten],

61: þæt hys yrþ si gefriþod [wið ealra feonda gehwæne],

62: and heo si geborgen [wið ealra bealwa gehwylc],

60: and his halige, þe on heofonum synt,

The question then is whether the Corvey Abbey charm ever actually existed, and thus provides our first independent account of a female deity with a name similar to Bede's goddess *Eostre*, or was it, as most authorities now suspect, a fabricated text largely derived from the authentic *Æcerbot* charm? Hocker was a known associate of Jacob Grimm and would surely have been aware of his comments on the *Æcerbot*, where Grimm suggested that in the invocation '*erce, erce, erce, eordhan modor...* it would surely be more correct to write *Eorce*' (Grimm 1835, 154; Stallybrass 1882, 253). With this knowledge we begin to see a process by which the 'Corvey' invocation could have been developed (Old English *Erce* > Grimm **Eorce* > Hocker **Eostar*), and, if they had assumed that the British Library manuscript containing the *Æcerbot* and the *Heliand* had originally come from Corvey Abbey, it would go a long way to explaining the origin of Hocker and Montanus' claims. Another example in this type of literature is an Old High German lullaby, whose discovery was announced in 1859 by Georg Zappert, a collector of medieval literature in Vienna. The manuscript was said to have found in the spine of a later book, and was claimed to contain a ninth- or tenth-century poem with various pre-Christian mythological references. Zappert reorganised the manuscript text into seven lines of Old High German alliterative verse, with his fourth line making reference to Ostara leaving honey and sweet eggs for the child:

Ostra stelit chinde honac egir suoziu. (manuscript, Zappert 1859, 3)

Ostârâ stellit chinde, honak egir suozziu. (reconstruction, Zappert 1859, 4)

The manuscript is considered to be a forgery by many experts who have examined it, with the most recent assessment, carried out by Cyril Edwards, concluding that the various forms of evidence (materials, palaeography, language and content) all point towards it being a fabrication (Edwards 2002, 161). Furthermore, the connection made between Ostara and sweet eggs looks highly suspect (see chapters 4 and 6).

During the later part of the nineteenth century, references to Ostara began to appear more widely in German art, literature, music and science. Examples include illustrations for books on Germanic mythology (see figures 4 and 5), such as Carl Emil Doepler's (1824–1905) depiction of the Norse goddess 'Frigg as Ostara' in classical Graeco-Roman dress, with female attendants and a hare nesting eggs at her feet (Wägner 1882, 124); and Johannes Gehrts' (1855–1921) depiction of a radiant 'Ostara' flying high in the sky, accompanied by a hare, stork and other spring birds, while her pagan Germanic worshippers celebrate below (Dahn 1885, 192). A similarly dressed image of Ostara walking across an upland landscape appears on a postcard produced by the *Bund der Deutschen in Böhmen* (Association of Germans in Bohemia), a society formed in 1894 to represent the interests of the (former) German-speaking minority in Bohemia's Sudetenland (today within the Czech Republic). The postcard was one of a series they produced for the months of the year, with the fourth (April) entitled *Ostermond: Ostara*. Similar imagery was likewise used by the Ostara students association at Freistadt in Austria, which was also founded in 1894. In the world of popular dance music Ostara was the theme for a waltz (*Ostara-Wals*) by the Dutch composer J.A. van der Linde, with the music score cover bearing an Art Nouveau image of the rising sun (Van der Linde, 1915). While in the realm of science, the goddess name was given to a

Figure 4. Carl Emil Doepler's (1824–1905) depiction of the Norse goddess 'Frigg as Ostara' first published in 1882.

Figure 5. Johannes Gehrts' (1855–1921) depiction of a radiant Ostara above her Germanic followers, published in 1885.

background asteroid from the inner region of the asteroid belt, by the German astronomer Max Wolf working at the Heidelberg Observatory in 1892 (Minor Planet Center: 343 Ostara).

However, the reconstructed goddess *Ostara* also has a somewhat more sinister history. The *Völkisch* movement had a significant influence not only in Germany, but throughout the German-speaking regions of Europe, and particularly in neighbouring Austria. Here two notable individuals promoted the spurious claim that the country's name *Österreich* was derived from their Germanic ancestors' worship of the goddess Ostara. Guido Karl Anton List (1848–1919) or 'Guido von List' was an Austrian writer and occultist, who promoted a neopagan movement known as Wotanism (after the god Wotan/Woden), in which he claimed to be reviving the ancient religion of the German 'race' with a set of teachings he called Armanism (Goodrick-Clarke 2004, 33–89). List wrote epic poems to advance his ideas, with one such poem entitled *Ostaras Einzug* (Ostara's entry) being published in the daily newspaper *Ostdeutsche Rundschau* in 1896, and soon after set to music by Karl Sipek for a special recital by the Wiedner Sängerbund (choir) in south Vienna (List 1896, 1–3; Goodrick-Clarke 2004, 40). At the conclusion of this epic poem Wotan's daughter Ostara enters Ostarland (Austria), the land dedicated to her, and implores her Germanic people to rise up and free themselves from oppression:

> *Und hell im Liede jubelt's die Liebe durch das Land,*
> *Wie dort am Hermannskogel die hehre Göttin stand,*
> *Wie dort am Hermannskogel beglückt ihr Ostarland,*
> *Die holde Wuotanstochter mit Spruch und Segenshand.*

And in bright song love rejoices through the land,
How there on Hermann's hill the noble goddess did stand,
How there on Hermann's hill she gladdened her Ostarland,
The beloved Wotan's daughter with speech and blessing hand.

Und also will ich künden, was Ostara dort sang,

Wie Ostarlandes Segen im Zauberliede klang;

So höret es denn Alle, aus Heimdold's Hochgeschlecht,

Vernehmt der Göttin Heilsrath, und werdet ihm gerecht!

And so I will tell you, what Ostara there sang,

How Ostarland's blessing in the magic-songs rang;

So then all hear it, from Heimdold's noble family,

Hark the Goddess' wise counsel, and follow it rightly!

(Extract from Ostaras Einzug (List 1896, 3) with author's translation.)

List's ideas were absorbed and expanded upon by Adolf Josef Lanz (1874–1954), the self-titled 'Jörg Lanz von Liebenfels' (Goodrick-Clarke 2004, 90-122). Lanz was a former Cistercian monk and founder of the right-wing Austrian magazine *Ostara* (1905–1917, reissued 1926-1931), in which he published a mix of *völkisch*, esoteric, racist and anti-Semitic theories, which he collectively termed Ariosophy (see figure 6). Readers of *Ostara* are alleged to have included Adolf Hitler while living in Vienna. Whether this is true or not is difficult to say. Nevertheless, many of the ideas contained in the magazines clearly anticipated, if not directly influenced, later Nazi ideology. In 1919 when Hitler joined the *Deutsche Arbeiterpartei* (forerunner of the *Nationalsozialistische Deutsche Arbeiterpartei* or Nazi Party) one on the many allied right-wing nationalist groups, that was also under surveillance by the Munich authorities, was the *Ostara-Bund* or 'Ostara League' (Deuerlein 1959, 245). In both Germany and Austria these *völkisch* groups and writers would inspire a pseudo-archaeology intent on finding evidence to prove, rather than test, their theories, with one of its most influential advocates being Wilhelm Teudt (1860–1942). His main work entitled *Germanische Heiligtümer* (Germanic

OSTARA

Nr. 1

Die Oſtara und das Reich der Blonden

Von J. Lanz-Liebenfels

Als Handſchrift gedruckt in 2. Auflage, Wien 1930
Copyright by J. Lanz v. Liebenfels, Wien 1922

Figure 6. Cover of Ostara magazine (reprint of first issue) published in Vienna by Jörg Lanz von Liebenfels in 1930.

Sanctuaries) was first published in 1929 and interpreted a wide range of natural geological features and monuments of different periods as evidence of an ancient and advanced Germanic civilisation (Teudt 1931)—in particular those related to the ancient rock formation the Externsteine. In this quest Teudt revisited the late seventeenth-century work of Ernst Wasserbach, who had suggested that the forests and groves at Kohlstädt were dedicated to the Gods, with a sanctuary of the goddess *Ostera* near Oesterholz (Wassserbach 1698, 7; Teudt 1931, 92–94). In his attempt to locate the temple or sanctuary site, Teudt focused on an area of extensive woodland to the north-west of Oesterholz containing various prehistoric burial mounds and earthworks known as the *Lauen* (Eckelau, Lindelau, Königslau and Langelau). With the help of a local resident, Teudt identified a group of three Bronze Age burial mounds that were said to have been the historic location for Easter bonfires (*Osterfeuer*). Given this folkloric association and based on the close proximity of the three barrows, Teudt then compared them to the three great mounds at Gamla Uppsala in Sweden, containing royal burials dating from the fifth to sixth century AD, and declared them to be a similar 'three hill sanctuary' (*dreihügelheiligtum*) dedicated to the goddess Ostara (Teudt 1931, 142–150). However, Teudt's ideas did not go unchallenged, with Friedrich Langewiesche (1931) deconstructing his many dubious interpretations, creative illustrations and chronological impossibilities.

In 1933 Adolf Hitler and the Nazi party came to power in Germany, which saw an end to democracy and the Weimar Republic, with the party taking ever greater control of the German state, its institutions, and wider society. One of the first areas to come under Nazi control was the supply of information, whether through published books, newspapers and magazine, or through film and radio. In order to achieve this, the 'Ministry for Public Enlightenment and Propaganda' was established under the propaganda minister Joseph Goebbels. One of the ministry's international outlets was the Terramare Office (publishers) in Berlin, which in 1934 released an illustrated English language book written by the English author and poet Ethel Talbot Scheffauer (1888–1976) entitled *Eastertide in Germany*. This, and similar publications, sought to normalise the Nazi state and present the country in a more positive light to world audiences, by covering various aspects of German life, including its Easter traditions:

> Some trace a connection between Ostara, goddess of Spring, the same whom the Venerable Bede mentions as Eostrae, or Easter, and some far-off Egyptian Venus to whom the hare, the symbol of fruitfulness, was sacred... As the hare and the Easter egg are said to be sacred to Ostara, so the Easter fires, which should be built of his own oak, are said to be in honour of Donar or Thor, the red-haired paladin who has slain the Giant Winter with his great hammer and in whose fires red-haired animals, squirrels and foxes, were formerly sacrificed, The last trace of the sacrifice is the Easter bone-burning which is still a feature of the beacons in some parts of the country. (Scheffauer 1934, 4 and 8)

In the above extract Scheffauer introduces the Easter fire (*Oster-feuer*) tradition where throughout Germany huge bonfires are set alight on either Holy Saturday or Easter Sunday, often on high ground with the earliest accounts dating back to the sixteenth century. The flame is kindled during the Easter vigil and is used to light the Easter Candle (*osterkerze*) in the local parish church. In the town of Lügde an even more spectacular tradition known as the *Osterräderlauf* or 'Easter-wheel-run' is maintained. As night falls on Easter Sunday, six enormous oak wheels (*Osterräder*) are filled with straw, set ablaze and rolled down the slopes of the *Os-terberg* or 'Easter-mountain'. Each wheel has a unique Christian motto carved into its rim. Though often said to be of pagan origin, the age of the custom is difficult to establish. Local tradition has it that Charlemagne stayed at Lügde for the Christmas of 784 AD, and when told of the *Osterräder* he allowed them to continue pro-vided they were run in celebration of Christ's resurrection. In

Scheffauer's book she provides a description of the event sometime between 1930 and 1934:

> A gloriously picturesque variant of the Easter fire are the Easter wheels which are set rolling down the height that rises behind the village of Lügde, near Bad Pyrmont. These wheels represent perhaps the most ancient of all the Easter customs, portraying, as they do, the living wheel of the sun. They are massive affairs of oak, each weighing nearly half a ton. For days before, the Brotherhood of the Wheel go from house to house all over the neighbourhood collecting straw to fill the wheels. At midday on Easter Sunday, the wheels and straw are drawn in procession through the village and up on to the Easter Hill. Here much remains to be done. A strong stake must be driven into each side of each wheel to steady it in its mad downward course. Withy withes are cut and twisted into suppleness to bind the straw into sheaves. The great wheels are stuffed with as much straw as possible. When all is prepared, the brotherhood return to the town and their Easter feast, leaving only a couple of watchmen on the hill. At last twilight comes. The entire population, reinforced by many strangers, assembles at the foot of the hill. Shots give the signal for the departure of the first wheel. The straw flames up, pitchforks drive the wheel on its fiery course.
>
> It sways from side to side, always thrust back into its path by the long stakes at its sides. At first it stumbles clumsily along, then it rolls faster and faster, takes a wild spring over a break in the hillside, rights itself, sprays out a very rain of sparks and rolls thunderously on, leaving a long glowing ribbon of light behind it. At last it lands and the brethren rush to free the precious wheel from the last remnants of burning straw. For the wheel is a valuable possession. Well-treated, it lasts for twenty or thirty years. Now and then, of course, a new one must be provided. Decked with wreaths of flowers and furnished with a motto, the

Figure 7. Osterräder (Easter-wheel) with Ostara motto and Osterdechen song (1929/1930) on a locally printed postcard (reproduced courtesy of Andreas Marz, Osterdechen, Lügde).

new wheel of the sun is solemnly installed among its fellows. (Scheffauer 1934, 11–12)

Scheffauer goes on to explain that the new wheel in 1930 was inscribed with a motto making reference to the goddess Ostara. This flaming-wheel was illustrated on a locally printed poster and postcard (see figure 7), along with the song of the *Osterdechen* or guardians of this Easter tradition, which also made reference to Ostara (Vesting 1929):

"Lügde", die Stadt der Osterräder!	**"Lügde", the town of the Easter-wheels!**
Mich tat man das: Osterrad taufen!	They baptised me: Easter-wheel deep!
Meine Vorfahr'n mußten für die Ostera laufen.	My forebears must for Ostara leap.
Osterdechen-Gesang	**The Easter-guardians Song**
(Aus dem Osterräder von Otto Vesting)	(About the Easter-wheels by Otto Vesting)
Seht da den hohen Osterberg,	See there the high Easter-mountain,
Auf dem die Dechen hausen.	On which the Guardians dwell.
Des Abends wenn es dunkel wird,	At evening when it gets dark,
Die Räder runter laufen.	The wheels they run down.
Hebt Eure Häupter froh empor	Lift up your heads with joy
Und singet mit dem Dechenchor:	And sing with the Guardian-choir:
"Triumph der alten Sitte!"	"Triumph of the old custom!"
So war's wohl schon vor tausend Jahr	So it was a thousand years ago
Bei unsern alten Vätern.	With our forefathers.
Das Feuerrad, es galt fürwahr	The fire-wheel, it was true
Hier zu der Sonnenwende.	Here at the solstice.
Sie waren Heiden dazumal,	They were heathens at that time,
Drum riefen Sie die Ostera	So they called to Ostara
Um ihren Segen an!	For her blessing!
Doch da wir alle Christen sind,	But since we are all Christians,
Und diese Sitte pflegen,	And this custom we maintain,
So flehn am ersten Ostertag	So pray on the first day of Easter
Wir auch um Gottes Segen.	We too for God's blessing.
Die Feuerräder laufen dann	The fire-wheels then run
Vom Berge ins Mariental	From the mountains into the Mariental
Es sind die "Osterräder"!	They are the "Easter-wheels"!

In 1934 the *Osterräderlauf* became the focus of Nazi attention. The ancient German past was to be glorified by 'reconnecting' the custom with its pagan origins in celebration of the spring goddess

Ostara. An additional seventh wheel carried a motto in praise of the Third Reich, while two hundred SS torchbearers formed a huge blazing swastika on the slopes of the *Osterberg*. Nevertheless, many in Lügde were opposed to the Nazis paganising their Christian folk custom, and in protest erected a large cross on the mountain in 1935, which stands there today (Osterdechenverein Lügde 2024). Furthermore, the *Osterräderlauf* appear to be part of a much wider European tradition, as similar midsummer fire wheels are recorded in fourth-century France, fifteenth-century Gloucestershire, and nineteenth-century Devon and Glamorgan (Hutton, 1996, 311), and still form part of the Latvian midsummer festival of *Jani* (Feast of St John the Baptist).

The Nazis' exploitation of this and other German folk traditions is well documented, along with their abuse of Germanic mythology and heroic legend (Goodrick-Clarke 2004, 177-191). However, their ideas had not suddenly appeared, but had emerged over time from the art, music and literature of the German romantic and nationalist movement. Many of the supposed Ostara place names containing the initial elements *oster-* or *osten-* may simply relate to their geography and mean 'east' or 'eastern', particularly those with corresponding *wester-* or *westen-* forms of the same place name. This would include Wasserbach (1698) and Teudt's (1929) suggested sanctuary site at Oesterholz near Kohlstädt, given the existence of numerous etymological parallels, including a Westenholz near Delbrück some 25 kilometres to the south-west. It is also true of Rathlef's (1766) Osterberg near Nienburg, with corresponding Westerberg hill names at Lamstedt in Lower Saxony and Baumberge in North Rhine-Westphalia. Nevertheless, the name *Osterberg* could also indicate hills and high ground where the annual Easter (Paschal) bonfires were built, which appears to be the case at Lügde where the lighting of a large *Osterfeuer* precedes the release of the six *Osterräder*. These Easter fires are clearly linked to the fires kindled during the Easter vigil in Western Christian church (Catholic, Lutheran and Anglican), which in the medieval period would have taken place on the same day (using Julian calendar) that the Eastern Orthodox church celebrates the 'miraculous' appearance of the Holy Fire from Jesus' tomb (at the Church of the Holy Sepulchre) in Jerusalem. While Christian syncretism with earlier pagan fire traditions cannot be ruled out, there is no evidence to connect these German place names or Easter-fire traditions to a reconstructed goddess Ostara. Likewise, the Corvey Abbey charm (Hocker 1853, 224; Montanus 1858, 28) and Old High German lullaby (Zappert 1859, 3–4), with their references to Ostara, would appear to be the creations of Jacob Grimm's associates and contemporaries, eager to provide evidence in support of his theories.

CHAPTER 8

Neopagans, Witches and Wiccans:
Ostara and the Wheel of the Year

Thus far we have demonstrated that the Feast of the Resurrection's timing (being related to the Jewish Passover), name in most languages (descending from the Passover's Hebrew and Aramaic names) and most common symbol (the egg), were almost certainly not 'stolen' or appropriated by Christians from any ancient north European pagan tradition. We have also demonstrated that the hare or rabbit is a relatively recent addition to the secular games and activities associated with the Paschal festival, appearing long after the last pagans in Europe were converted to Christianity. But where could such received wisdom (now widespread on the internet) have originated? Most people will become aware of these annual 'Ostara versus Easter' appropriation claims from members of what is now the world's largest neopagan religion: Wicca. The spring (vernal) equinox usually falls on either the 20th or 21st of March and is celebrated by Wiccans as the 'Sabbat of Ostara', one of the eight festivals in their 'Wheel of the Year'. While many of its elements are indeed ancient, the year they now follow is a composite creation of far more recent origin. To understand how this Wiccan year came into existence, and how it came to include a festival named after Grimm's reconstructed goddess *Ostara*, we need to start by looking at its earliest elements.

The longest-spoken languages in Britain and Ireland are descendants of the Celtic branch of the Indo-European family: Brittonic or P-Celtic (Welsh and Cornish) and Goidelic or Q-Celtic (Irish, Manx and Scottish Gaelic). The Celts (Greek Κελτοί) were first recorded in the fifth century BC by the Greek historian Herodotus, who locates them in the area of the upper Danube (Selincourt, 1954, 142). Later Roman historians referred to a number of peoples within their empire as being either Celts or Gauls, and located them in what is now northern Italy, France, Spain and Portugal. Nineteenth-century archaeologists attempted to find evidence of these early Celts in central Europe, and identified two possible candidates: The Bronze Age *Hallstatt* culture discovered in Austria, and the Iron Age *La Tène* culture discovered in Switzerland (Renfrew 1987, 211–249). With the subsequent discovery of this material culture (artefacts) across western Europe, it was assumed that an Iron Age migration had brought the Celtic people and their language to Britain and Ireland (Cunliffe 1997). This was the long-held view until archaeologists began to question the lack of evidence for any such migration (James 1999). Recent advances in ancient DNA analysis now suggest that this migration may have occurred sometime earlier in the Bronze Age (Patterson et al. 2022). However, it is important to note that the Celtic language group was only defined by that name at the beginning of the eighteenth century, by Edward Lhuyd who was then curator of the Ashmolean Museum in Oxford (Lhuyd 1707), and its relationship to these archaeological cultures is the still the subject of much debate. Nevertheless, at their greatest extent, what we now call the Celtic languages were spoken throughout much of central and western Europe, including Britain and Ireland.

The following passage is taken from an early medieval collection of Irish heroic tales, commonly known as the *Ulster Cycle*:

> 'Ní rúalae a mag sa,' ol sí, 'nad écmonga benn Súain meic Roiscmilc ó samsúan co hoímelc, ó oímelc co beltine, co brón trogain ó beltine.'
> (Van Hemel 1978, 31–32)

'No man will travel this country,' she said, 'who has not gone sleepless from Samain to Imbolc, from Imbolc to Beltane, and from Beltane to Brón Trogain.' (based on Kinsella 1970, 27)

During the wooing of Emer (*Tochmarc Emire*) by the hero Cúchulainn, he is required to go without sleep for a whole year before she will agree to marry him. In describing that year Emer provides the earliest account of all four Old Irish festivals that marked the cross-quarter days of the solar year, each occurring roughly halfway between one of the solstices and one of the equinoxes. These festivals, which marked the changing of the seasons, were subsequently fixed as the first days of February, May, August and November (see table 16). In later sources *Brón Trogain* (earth's sorrowing autumn) was known by the name *Lúgnasad*, while *Imbolc* became the feast day of St Bridget (Irish *Naomh Bríde*). Today they survive as the month names for May, August and November in the modern Goidelic (Gaelic) languages, and mark the beginnings of the old calendar terms or quarters in Scotland and Ireland.

Old Irish	Irish / Gaeilge	Manx Gaelic	Scottish Gaelic	Interpretation
Imbolc	(Bride)	(Breeshey)	(Brighde)	Ewes' milking (start of spring)
Beltane	Bealtaine	Boaldyn	Bealltainn	Bright fire (start of summer)
Lúgnasad	Lúnasa	Luanistyn	Lùnasdal	Lug's festival (start of autumn)
Samain	Samhna	Sauin	Samhainn	Summer's end (start of winter)

Table 16. Old Irish and Gaelic cross-quarter days.

In the nineteenth century these early Irish festivals were rediscovered by folklorists and academics such as Sir James Frazer (1854-1941), who between 1890 and 1915 published his thirteen-volume work *The Golden Bough*, a monumental study in comparative folklore, magic, and religion, with a widely available abridgement coming out in 1922. Frazer's study attempted to reconstruct a pre-Christian solar year, which was believed to have included the winter and summer solstices, the spring and autumn equinoxes, and at least two of the Old Irish festivals that marked the changing seasons (*Beltane* and *Samain*). In addition to which it was thought that bonfires had played a central role within these festivals, giving rise to the concept of the 'Fire Festivals' (Frazer 1922, 609–641). While Frazer's work has now been largely rejected by modern academics, including the so-called 'Celtic Calendar' that it inspired (Hutton 1996, 408-411), it was very influential in framing both academic and popular understandings of our pagan past during the early to mid-twentieth century; and it is in this period that we see the emergence of modern pagan witchcraft or Wicca, which is today the world's largest and most widespread neopagan religion. The history of the modern Druids, Wiccans and other related neopagan groups has been explored in great detail by Ronald Hutton (2001, 2008 and 2009), and will only be touched upon here in as much as it relates to the Wiccan festivals named after the goddesses *Eostre* and/or *Ostara*.

The person credited with either founding the Wicca religion, or bringing its existence and the 'survival' of ancient witchcraft to wider public attention (according to his own narrative), was the retired British civil servant (government worker) Gerald Gardner (1884–1964). The founding text of the syncretic pagan religion that Gardner promoted was his book *Witchcraft Today* published in 1954, in which he described the four Gaelic (Old Irish) 'fire festivals' and two solstices (including Yule) as the Wiccans' principal festivals or 'sabbats' (Hutton 2008, 258–259):

> I have seen one very interesting ceremony: the Cauldron of Regeneration and the Dance of the Wheel, or Yule, to cause the sun to be reborn, or summer to return. This in theory should be on December 22, but nowadays it is held on the nearest day to that date that is convenient for the members. (Gardner 1954, 24)

> It is, I think, fairly well known that witches observed four great festivals: May eve, August eve, November eve (Hallowe'en) and February eve. These seem to correspond to the divisions of the ancient Gaelic year by the four fire festivals of Samhaim or

Samhuin (November 1), Brigid (February 1), Bealteine or Beltene (May 1) and Lugnasadh (August 1). The festivals corresponding to midwinter and midsummer were both said to have been founded in honour of female deities: Brigid is a very ancient goddess of home-crafts and the hearth, Lugnasadh was founded by Lugaidh in honour of his 'nurse' Taillte. (Gardner 1954, 130)

The two decades that followed its publication saw the development of the 'Counter Culture' among the post-war generation, starting in America and then spreading across the western world. This was accompanied by a growing interest in alternative forms of spirituality, including various eastern religions and philosophies, esoteric and occult beliefs, and nature-centred forms of paganism. This was particularly true in California, where much of the counter-culture movement began, and where Gardner's ideas found a highly receptive audience. It was here in 1974 that the Wiccan poet and writer Aidan Kelly introduced terms for the unnamed sabbats on equinoxes and summer solstice (Ostara, Litha and Mabon), which he elaborates on in a more recent online blog:

Back in 1974, I was putting together a 'Pagan-Craft' calendar... We have Gaelic names for the four Celtic holidays. It offended my aesthetic sensibilities that there seemed to be no Pagan names for the summer solstice or the fall equinox equivalent to Yule or Beltane—so I decided to supply them. The spring equinox was almost a nonissue. The Venerable Bede says that it was sacred to a Saxon Goddess, Ostara or Eostre, from whom we get the name 'Easter'... Summer was also rather easy. The Saxon calendar described by Bede was lunisolar... The last and first months in the calendar were named Foreyule and Afteryule, respectively, and obviously framed the holiday of Yule. The sixth and seventh months were named

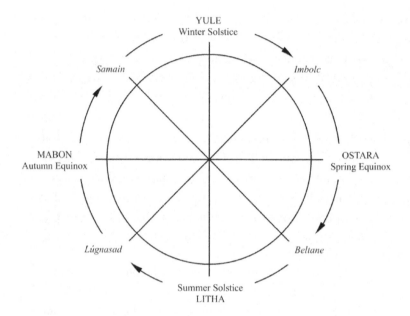

Figure 8. Diagrammatic representation of the Wiccan 'Wheel of the Year' (drawn by the author).

Forelitha and Afterlitha... by analogy with Yule, the summer solstice must have been called Litha (I later discovered that Tolkien
had figured this out also)... the fall equinox was special to the Saxons also. But what was its name?... I could not find one in
Germanic or Gaelic literature, but there was one in the Welsh, in
the Mabinogion collection, the story of Mabon ap Modron (which
translates as 'Son of the Mother'), whom Gwydion rescues from
the underworld... so I picked 'Mabon' as the name for the holiday
in my calendar... I sent a copy of the calendar to Oberon (then still
Tim), who liked these new names and began using them in Green
Egg, whence they passed into the national Pagan vocabulary. (Kelly
2017)

The eight-spoke Wheel of the Year (see figure 8 and table 17) was
now complete, and it was promoted through the widely-read neopagan magazine *Green Egg* (1968–1976 and 1982 onwards), which
was produced by the Wiccan religious leader Oberon (Tim Zell).
Various books and publications from America then made these new
festival names popular back in Britain, where they have become permanent features of the Wiccan calendar (Hutton 2008, 261–262).
Nevertheless, it is interesting to note that in Kelly's (2017) blog he
appears to be using Tolkien's *Lord of the Rings* (Shire Calendar) renderings of Bede's month names (Afteryule, Solmath, Rethe, Astron,
Thrimidge, Forelithe, Afterlithe, Wedmath, Halimath, Winterfilth,
Blotmath, and Foreyule), rather than Bede's original spellings (Tolkien 1955, appendix D). This begs the question—as previously posed
by Hutton (2008, 260)—whether Kelly's 'Saxon' names (Ostara and
Litha) were more influenced by those of Grimm (Ostara) and Tolkien (Lithe), than they were by Bede's original names? Whether this
is true or not, the festival names introduced by Kelly, and Ostara in
particular, are now widely used in numerous modern pagan and hea-
then traditions (Cusack 2007).

Wiccan Year	Date	Cultural and Linguistic Origin	Introduced
Yule	21 December	Old English *Geola* (midwinter or winter solstice)	Gardner 1954
Imbolc	1 February	Old Irish quarter day (beginning of spring)	Gardner 1954
Ostara	21 March	Old English *Eostre* > Jacob Grimm (1835) *Ostara	Kelly 1974
Beltane	1 May	Old Irish quarter day (beginning of summer)	Gardner 1954
Litha	21 June	Old English *Litha* (midsummer or summer solstice)	Kelly 1974
Lúgnasad	1 August	Old Irish quarter day (beginning of autumn)	Gardner 1954
Mabon	22 September	Mabinogion *Mabon ap Modron* (son of the mother)	Kelly 1974
Samain	1 November	Old Irish quarter day (beginning of winter)	Gardner 1954

Table 17. Wiccan 'Wheel of the Year' with festival origins and modern provenances.

Common misconceptions

Two very common misconceptions regarding the etymology of Bede's goddess *Eostre* have resulted from false connections made with similar sounding names:

The first misconception is that the goddess' name derives from the same root as the female hormone Oestrogen, which if viewed from the perspective of many goddess-centred neopagans provides a convenient explanation. However, the hormone name derives from a very different classical root (Greek οἶστρος > Latin *oestrus*) originally meaning 'gadfly' or 'frenzy', and only gained its modern meaning, in relation to the female fertility cycle, during the late sixteenth century. It was not until the early twentieth century that the hormone was first isolated and subsequently named Oestrogen or Estrogen (from the Latin *oestrus* + *gen*).

The second misconception is that the name derives from an ancient Semitic goddess known to the Babylonians and Assyrians as *Ishtar*, and to the Phoenicians and Canaanites as *Astarte* (Biblical *Ashtoreth*, I Kings 11:5). Her cult was spread throughout the Mediterranean by the Phoenicians, and was adopted by the Greeks and Romans who associated her with their native goddesses Aphrodite and Venus. Interestingly, this supposed connection with *Eostre* is not a new idea, with a similar conclusion having been reached by German geographer and historian Philipp Clüver in his *Germaniae Antiquae* (Clüver 1616, 237). Furthermore, within 26 miles (40 kilometres) of Bede's monastery at Jarrow is the Roman fort of Corbridge (*Corstopitum*), where an altar dedicated to *Astarte* was discovered, the only such example from Roman Britain (Collingwood and Wright, 1965, no. 1124):

> Greek inscription: Αστ[αρ]της βωμον μ εσορας Πουλχερ μ ανεθηκεν

> Translation: Astarte's altar, you see me, Poulcher placed me.

However, we must exercise caution, since more than four hundred years separate Bede's reference to *Eostre* and this isolated altar to *Astarte* (now in the Tullie House Museum, Carlisle); and more importantly, all of Bede's month names appear to have Indo-European (Germanic) roots, with no known relationship to the Semitic goddess's name.

CHAPTER 9

The *Matronae Austriahenae*:
Pan-Tribal Mothers or Local Cult?

One of the criticisms most often levelled against Bede and his account of goddess *Eostre* is that he provides the only written evidence for this Anglo-Saxon deity. Nevertheless, a similar goddess name does exist on a group of Roman altar stones from the Lower Rhine region of north-west Germany, in what was the Roman province of Germania Inferior. These altars are dedicated to native mother goddesses known as *Matres* or *Matronae*, who were often depicted as triple deities, and thought to bestow protection and good fortune on their followers. These Romanised matron cults appear to stem from an originally Gaulish (Celtic) tradition, with *Matrona* 'the great mother goddess' thought to have been the tutelary deity of the river Marne (described in Caesar's *Gallic Wars*, book 1, chapter 1). The word *matrona* means 'mother' in both Gaulish and Latin; and in Gaulish the suffix *-ona/-onos* usually signifies a deity name. Altars dedicated to similar goddesses have been found in northern Italy, France, Spain and Britain. In these former Roman provinces the matrons' standard (plural) form of address is often followed by a Celtic name or epithet, whereas in the Lower Rhine many appear to have Germanic names (Todd 1992, 105), such as the *Matronae Alagabiae* (all-giving mothers) found on altar stones at Bürgel. Others were named after known

107

Germanic tribes, like the *Matres Frisavae* and *Matres Suebae* found at Xanten and Cologne, or were worshipped at dedicated temple sites, like the *Matronae Vacallinehae* at Pesch and the *Matronae Aufaniae* at Nettersheim. However, the altar stones that are most relevant to our discussion of *Eostre* were dedicated to mother goddesses known as the *Matronae Austriahenae*.

In April 1958, numerous, mostly broken, Roman altar stones and architectural fragments were discovered at Morken-Harff near Bedburg, 30 kilometres north-west of Cologne (Kolbe 1960, 50–53). The initial find, of three complete altar stones, was made by local school children at the edge of an open-caste brown coal mine (Frimmersdorf Roddergrube), 150 metres east of the parish church of Harff on the east bank of the river Erft. In the following days the site was excavated by staff of Rheinische Landesmuseum, who retrieved another complete altar stone, over five hundred altar fragments, and around sixty architectural fragments (Rheinisches Landesmuseum, Bonn, accession numbers 1958, 682–999). These finds were located approximately two metres below the existing ground surface, mixed with a similar quantity of amorphous stone blocks, and packed into a narrow strip (30 × 5 metres) running east to west across the low-lying area. This structure was logically interpreted as a late Roman or early medieval ford through the wetlands of the Erft valley, with the stones thought to have been brought from a nearby (unlocated) temple or shrine. Once analysed the retrieved material could be seen to comprise four intact altars, four reassembled altars, 90 partially reassembled altars, and 220 isolated altar fragments; this gave the total of 318 possible monuments, of which 155 had inscriptions (Kolbe 1960, 53–124). The stone altars were originally carved from single blocks of either sandstone or limestone, and can be dated to around 150–250 AD, with 154 of the altars thought to have been dedicated to the *Matronae Austriahenae* (see table 18). The Latin inscriptions are formulaic with the matron name being followed by the name of the person making the dedication, and then a series of standard phrases: *pro se et suis* (for himself and his family), *ex imperio ip-sarum* (by their command) and *votum solvit libens merito* (he willingly and deservedly fulfilled his vow). While none of the altar stones bear any images of the *Austriahenae*, the matron name clearly contains a first element (*austr-*) that if Germanic would be cognate with the goddess name *Eostre*. However, we must not jump to conclusions. While these two deity names may appear to derive from a common (Proto-Germanic) word meaning 'east' this does not necessarily mean that the two goddess concepts share a common origin. For example, in Old Norse mythology we find the name *Aus-tri* for one of the four cardinal dwarfs who support the sky (*Völuspá*, stanza 11). While the name clearly derives from the same linguistic root, the mythological or religious concept is quite different. Not-withstanding this cautionary advice, the inscriptions found at Morken-Harff now provide important comparative evidence in any assessment of Bede's goddess *Eostre*.

No.	Latin Inscription
1	[M]atronis [...]cifnis [A]uvacsis [...]lia v(otum) s(olvit) l(ibens) m(erito)
2	Matronis Austriahenis M(arcus) Antonius Sentius p(ro) s(e) et s(uis) l(ibens) m(erito)
3	Matronis Austriahenabus Q(uintus) Atilius Gemellus v(otum) s(olvit) l(ibens) m(erito)
4	Austriahenis Juli(us) Jus[ti]nus Verinus Paterna ex imp(erio) ips(arum) l(ibens) m(erito)
5	M(arcus) Julius Vassileni f(ilius) Leubo Matr[o]nis Austriatium v(otum) s(olvit) m(erito)
6	Matronis Austriahenabus Q(uintus) Lucretius Patro(n) pro se v(otum) s(olvit) l(ibens) m(erito)
7	Matronis Austriahenis M(arcus) M(arius) Celsus ex imperio ipsarum s(olvit) l(ibens) m(erito)
8	Matronis Austriahen[a]bus T(itus) Quartio pro se et suis v(otum) s(olvit) l(ibens) m(erito)
9	Matronis [Au]striahenabus [...

Table 18. Principal examples of the Morken-Harff inscriptions discovered in 1958 (Kolbe 1960, nos. 1–9; Merlin 1962, nos. 98–106).

The archaeological evidence from Morken-Harff strongly sug-gests that a shrine or cult centre had existed in the vicinity, like the temple sites at Pesch and Nettersheim. Unfortunately, the time to test this theory has long since past, as the village of Morken-Harff (and its underlying deposits) no longer exists, having been levelled for further open-cast mining in the 1960s. Nevertheless, it is worth noting that the *Matronae Austriahenae* were not the only matron cult to have been discovered at Morken-Harff. In addition to one of the 1958 discoveries, which was dedicated to the *Matronae ...cifnae* (Kolb 1960, 53–54, no. 1), a group of five altars dedicated to the *Matronae Vatviae* (*Berhliahenae*) were found in 1943, approximately 350 metres north-west of the old church tower in Morken, during an earlier expansion of the brown coal mine (Nesselhauf and Lieb 1959, 205–206, nos. 232–236).

The matron cults of the Lower Rhine region, and the *Matronae Austriahenae* in particular, have played a central part in Philip Shaw's theorising on the goddess *Eostre* (Shaw 2011, 40–48, 52–53, and 61–64). Shaw devotes a large part of his work to these goddesses, which he sees as native cults that had undergone a process of Romanisation (Shaw 2011, 43). Shaw makes specific reference to a study carried out by Günter Neumann in 1987, which found that the various matron names appearing in the Latin votive inscriptions of Germania Inferior appear to have either Germanic or Celtic origins (Neumann 2008, 256). Neumann undertook a detailed examination of 56 matron names or epithets, which he divided into four main categories: tribal or group names (ethnonyms), place or settlement names (toponyms), river or water names (hydronyms), and function or activity names (Neumann 2008, 260–64). Shaw similarly relies on a study by Ton Derks who suggests that these named matron cults were the result of marriages between local Ubian women and retired Roman soldiers (Derks 1998, 128–129). The area around Cologne had been settled by numerous Roman veterans, who were granted land and other special privileges, following the city's designation as a *colonia* in 50 AD. The Ubians (Latin *Ubii*) were a Germanic tribe who in 39 BC, due to their early collaboration with the Romans, were relocated from their original home on the east bank of the Rhine to the relative safety of the river's west bank, which lay within the Roman Empire. Roman funerary inscriptions discovered in Cologne indicate that many of the military veterans came from towns and cities in northern Italy, including *Bononia* (Bologna), *Ticinum* (Pavia) and *Veleia* (Carroll 2011, 226), in an area where votive inscriptions to a more generic cult of unnamed *Matronae* have been found (Derks 1998, figure 3.19, findspots B). Derks suggests that through family alliances and marriages this unnamed matron cult from northern Italy merged with a native (Ubian) ancestor cult, producing the cluster of named matron cults observed in the Lower Rhine region (Derks 1998, figure 3.19, findspots A); and that these cults 'kept their traditional native names: for the cult focussed on maternal ancestors' spreading across the region via social competition (Derks 1998, 128).

It is clear that many of these matron cults were named after social and ethnic groupings with possible pan-tribal, tribal or local (sub-tribal) affiliations, which Shaw suggests may reflect the dedicator's perceived distance from their home territory (see table 19). The narrower or more exclusive the matron cult or group name, the closer the dedicant to their ancestral homeland, and conversely, the broader or more inclusive the matron cult or group name, the further the dedicant from their ancestral homeland (Shaw 2011, 40 and 46).

Dedicators distant from home locality:	Pan-tribal/wide area name					
	Tribal name			Tribal name		
Dedicators within home locality:	Local/kin name	Local/kin name	Local/kin Name	Local/kin name	Local/kin Name	Local/kin name

Table 19. Diagrammatic hierarchy of matron names and localities (after Shaw 2011, table 1).

The *Austriahenae* epithet is thought to stem from an early West Germanic word *austra* meaning 'east' or 'eastern', which could offer an etymological analogue for the goddess name *Eostre* and theoretical Old English element *ēastor* (Shaw 2011, 52, 55, and

58). This explanation was first promoted by Leo Weisgerber in 1962, who compared the matron name to Germanic ethnic names like the *Austrogoti* (Ostrogoths) and *Austrasii* (Austrasians), and noted that of the many matron cults found between the rivers Rur (Roer) and Erft the *Matronae Austriahenae* was the north-eastern-most example, with a notable lack of examples to the west of the Rur (Weisgerber 1962, 132 and 134, notes 36 and 40). He also observed that the Erft's 'knee' (a major bend in the river) could have played a role in the naming process as a prominent eastern point in the local geography. Weisgerber's etymology is now widely accepted, with Neumann adding some further comparisons with Germanic place names including the North Sea island of Austera-via (recorded in Pliny's *Natural History*, book 4, section 97) and the seventh-century town of Austondorph, along with a number of Old English place names that are believed to contain the cog-nate element *ēastor* (Neumann 2008, 260–61) discussed in the next chapter.

Besides assessing the possible linguistic roots and meanings of the different matron names (conventionally presented in their nominative form), Neumann goes on to discuss their different suffixes (including -*ae*, -*iae*, -*nae*, -*hae*, -*nehae* and -*henae*), which convert the root word into an adjective (or attribute) following the standard matron title *matres* or *matronae* (Neumann 2008, 256–57). While these different word endings were clearly being used within Latin votive inscriptions, Neumann observes a difficulty in accounting for the the two consonants /h/ and /n/ in the longer forms, which he surmises could indicate an original (retained) Germanic suffix to which a Latin one was later added. Neumann then suggests that these longer word endings, and more specifi-cally the suffix -*henae*, are indicative of local toponyms and/or ethnonyms that gave rise to associated and similarly named matron cults (Neumann 2008, 264). Drawing on these ideas Shaw inter-

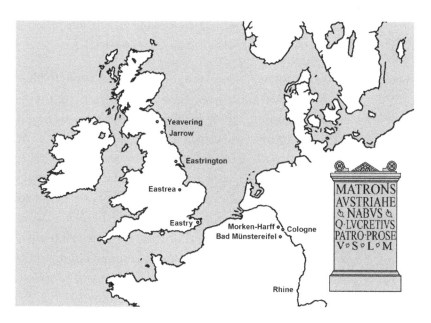

Figure 9. Map of north-west Europe showing the principal locations discussed in the final chapters, with inset example of the Morken-Harff altar stones (drawn by the author).

prets the *Matronae Austriahenae* as the 'eastern matrons' or 'matrons belonging to an eastern group of people', which he
characterises as the matron cult of a relatively small (sub-tribal)
group living within their home locality (Shaw 2011, 63):

> This group name may well relate in some way to local social
> geography, and we should therefore not see the name *Austriahe-*
> *nae* as related to the idea of migration from east of the Rhine,
> but rather as relating to local positioning in relation to other
> groups or areas in the region. (Shaw 2011, 63–64)

Nevertheless, two of Shaw's key assumptions warrant some further
consideration: firstly 'that the name *Austriahenae* refers to a relatively small-scale group and their locality' (Shaw 2011, 63), and
secondly 'that the matrons can be seen as evidence for an ancestor
cult that existed prior to the Romanisation of the area' (Shaw 2011,
43). With all but one of their votive inscriptions found at a single
location (and likely temple site) on the banks of the river Erft near
Morken-Harff (see figure 9), the *Matronae Austriahenae* were
clearly a localised cult. The single outlier was found in 1963–1964
having been incorporated into a nineteenth-century church altar
at Bad Münstereifel some 60 kilometres to the south of Morken-
Harff (Corbier 2001, 468, no. 1425; Biller 2001; Biller 2010, 235).
Although the matron name could reference a local 'eastern' people
or area, Shaw rightly cautions that 'We cannot hope to determine
exactly how such a group might have been defined as eastern, and
who might have been involved in this identification' (Shaw 2011,
63). Here we should perhaps note that there are no other matron
names thought to have been based on cardinal directions (north,
south or west). However, there are a number of altars from Roman
military sites in northern Britain dedicated to the *Matribus Trans-*
marinis or 'matrons across the sea' (Collingwood and Wright, 1965,
nos. 919, 920, 1030, 1224, 1318 and 1989). In these inscriptions
the Roman soldiers were dedicating altars to their ancestral mothers in their distant homelands across the *Oceanus Britannicus* or

Mare Britannicum (English Channel), and hence in a southerly direction, which could have a bearing on Shaw's interpretation of the *Matronae Austriahenae*. If we accept his reading of the name as 'matrons belonging to an eastern group of people', or as he later writes 'matrons of the easterners' (Shaw 2012), and then employ his same 'matron names and localities' hierarchy (see table 19), it could likewise be argued that the epithet was derived from a pan-tribal or wider area name, where the dedicants were remote from their ancestral 'eastern' homeland—an explanation that clearly accords with the historical accounts of the *Ubii* provided by Strabo (*Geography*, book 4, chapter 3, section 4) and Tacitus (*Germania*, chapter 28; *Annals*, book 12, chapter 27):

> The *Ubii* used to live opposite this region, across the Rhine, though by their own consent they were transferred by Agrippa to the country this side the Rhine. (Jones 1923, 231)

> Not even the *Ubii*, though they have earned the right to be a Roman colony, and prefer to be called 'Agrippinenses' from the name of their founder, blush to own their German origin: they originally came from beyond the river, and were placed in charge of the bank itself, after they had given proof of their loyalty, in order to block the way to others, not in order to be under supervision. (Peterson 1914, 303 and 305)

> Agrippina... arranged for the plantation of a colony of veterans in the Ubian town where she was born. The settlement received its title from her name; and, as chance would have it, it had been her grandfather Agrippa who extended Roman protection to the tribe on its migration across the Rhine. (Jackson 1937, 351)

This wider interpretation of the matron name (Sermon 2022) and has received support from Patrizia de Bernardo Stempel (2021, 124 and 2022, 300), who is one of the leading researchers in this field. In her recent work she has highlighted similar matron cults from the province of Germania Inferior whose names, in addition to providing the *Matronae Austriahenae* with strong etymological parallels, may also indicate the external (non-local) origin of their devotees (De Bernardo Stempel 2019, 138–42), including: the *Matronae Berguiahenae* from *Bergusia* (a place name and people in Spain and Gaul), the *Matronae Vesuniahenae* from *Vesunn(i)a* (a settlement and river in western Gaul), and the *Matronae Gesahenae* from *Gaisates* (a mercenary group from the Rhone valley). Surprisingly, Shaw fails to make any reference to the historic migration of the *Ubii* from their original homeland on the east bank of the Rhine. Instead he reiterates a theory by Derks that the Ubian people may have used different forms of address to distinguish their more local *matronae* from their wider tribal *matres* (Derks 1998, 127; Shaw 2011, 44). Nevertheless, Derks qualifies this suggestion by noting that 'inscriptions in which both terms occur alongside each other and dedications in which the customary form of address *matronae* is replaced by *matres*, make it clear that there was no sharp distinction' (Derks 1998, 120). This cautionary observation is likewise true of the Morken-Harff altars—while the majority were dedicated to *Matronis* (dative plural of *matronae*) at least two were dedicated to *Matribus* (dative plural of *matres*). Furthermore, the interchangeable use of the (dative plural) epithets *Austriahenis* and *Austriahenabus* would likewise indicate that there was no absolute division between these various forms of address (see table 20).

Form of Address	Prevalence	Foremost Examples
Matronis Austriahenis	Most common form	Kolbe 1960, nos 2, 4, and 7.
Matronis Austriahenabus	Second most common form	Kolbe 1960, nos 3, 6, and 8.
Matribus Austriahenis	Two occurrences	Kolbe 1960, nos 53 and 124.
Matronis Austriatium	One occurrence	Kolbe 1960, no. 5.

Table 20. Recorded forms of address for the *Matronae Austriahenae* on the altar stones found at Morken-Harff in 1958.

While not specifically addressing the question of its linguistic affiliation (whether Celtic or Germanic), De Bernardo Stempel categorises the *Austriahenae* epithet as an ethnonym or group name that developed in a similar manner to the *Berguiahenae* and *Vesuniahenae* (De Bernardo Stempel 2019, 142–43). Crucially, she calls into question Neumann's theory that the word ending -*henae* represents a Germanic-Latin suffixal conglutinate (De Bernardo Stempel 2019, 143), instead offering a simpler and more direct explanation. Firstly, De Bernardo Stempel cites various of Celtic and Romano-Celtic deity and personal names containing the suffixes -*genos* or -*gena* meaning 'born of', and secondly she observes that 'the rendering of a lenited [softened] Celtic *g* by means of *ch* or *h* is not unparalleled' in the early Celtic languages (De Bernardo Stempel 2019, 122–24). She therefore suggests that the matron names found in the Lower Rhine region were shaped by a Celtic word-formation process, where over time the plural suffix -*genae* developed into the recorded forms -*chenae*, -*henae* and -*enae* (De Bernardo Stempel 2019, 138–42).

So far we have noted that the *Matronae Austriahenae* were just one of many individually named matron cults that emerged among the Romanised population of Germania Inferior. These matron cults were undoubtedly shaped by broader Gallo-Roman religious traditions, as indicated by their use of Roman stone altars, votive Latin inscriptions, and their veneration of the *Matres* or *Matronae*. However, their individual matron names or epithets appear to include examples with Germanic (as well as Celtic) origins, including the name *Austriahenae* that is widely believed to descend from a common Germanic word meaning 'east' or 'eastern'. That being said, current research now suggests that their word endings (including the suffix -*henae*) are indicative of a Celtic (Gaulish) word-formation process and deity naming tradition. The Romanisation of this indigenous tradition, and the resulting emergence of matron cults with either Celtic or Germanic names, sits comfortably with what is known of the ethnic and linguistic history of the Lower Rhine region. The Roman invasion of the region (to the west of the river Rhine) commenced in 57 BC and formed part of the wider military campaigns lead by Julius Caesar during the conquest of Gaul. The indigenous groups within this area consisted of both Celtic and Germanic speaking peoples, with Roman settlements beginning to appear from the middle of the first century BC. Following the Germanic tribes' decisive victory over Varus and his legions in the Teutoburg forest in 9 AD, a series of interconnected forts was constructed along the Rhine providing a defensive eastern border (*Limes Germanicus*) to the Roman Empire. During this early period the Lower Rhine region sat within the greater Roman province of Gallia Belgica, when in 39 BC the Germanic-speaking *Ubii* (a tribe allied with Rome) were relocated from the east bank to the west bank of the river Rhine, with a new tribal capital at built at Cologne (Oppidum Ubiorum). Subsequently in 50 AD the Ubian city was elevated to the class of *colonia* (Colonia Claudia Ara Agrippinensium), a status requiring the resettlement of Roman military veterans from northern Italy, and in 85 AD the city was made capital of the recently created (separated) province of Germania Inferior. Therefore, when these named matron cults begin to appear—during the middle of the second century AD—the Ubian territory had already witnessed over two centuries of Roman, Gallo-Belgic (Celtic) and Germanic interaction. This cultural convergence and exchange may help to explain the different linguistic influences seen in the matron names of the Lower Rhine region: with the Romanisation (*interpretatio romana*) of a native Gaulish (Celtic) mother-goddess cult and deity-naming tradition, that was subsequently adopted by the Ubian (Germanic) settlers, who then attached both Germanic and Celtic epithets to their various matron cults.

Based on Derks' earlier work (Derks 1998, 119), Shaw observes that the matron cults of the Lower Rhine region with Germanic and Celtic epithets 'are commonest in the area inhabited by the *Ubii*' (Shaw 2011, 42–43). What is more, he subscribes to the theory that these matron cults are evidence of native ancestor cult that existed in the area before it came under Roman control (Shaw 2011, 43), and hence before 39 BC when the *Ubii* were relocated to this same area. However, it prompts the question whether this native (female) ancestor cult—for which we have no direct evidence—was: (a) present among the Germanic tribes living to the east of the Rhine, or (b) reflective of their wider Germanic deity-naming practices. A similar point was made by Malcolm Todd in his work on *The Early Germans*, in which he likewise noted the absence of evidence and uncertainty 'that triads of mother-goddesses were worshipped east of the Rhine' (Todd 1992, 105).

CHAPTER 8

CHAPTER 10

The Goddess *Eostre*:
Local Cult or Functional Deity?

One of the more recent (and somewhat influential) attempts to reassess Bede's account of the goddess *Eostre*, and the origins of the Easter festival name, has been provided by the linguist Philip Shaw (2011). Shaw finds no grounds to reject Bede's explanation that *Eosturmonath* was named after the pagan goddess, with the Christian festival name simply borrowed from the Anglo-Saxon month in which it frequently occurred; and he finds it difficult to imagine that Bede would have invented this story when he is so widely respected as 'a careful researcher' and one who was 'not prone to inventions of this sort' (Shaw 2012). Shaw's treatise on the goddess *Eostre* centres on Old English naming practices and those within the broader Germanic language group. Seeing analogies with cult of the *Matronae Austriahenae* in north-west Germany, while highlighting at least three related English place names, Shaw suggests that the cult of *Eostre* was a similarly localised religious tradition that may have originated in eastern Kent. Significantly, Shaw rejects the long-held view that *Eostre* was a 'functional' spring or dawn goddess, instead arguing that she was the tutelary goddess of an 'eastern' local community or socio-geographical grouping.

Shaw's reassessment of the linguistic evidence begins with a lost Old English word and name element *ēastor* meaning 'eastern', which he sees as providing the most likely origin of the names *Eostre* and *Eosturmonath*. While this name element is a linguistic reconstruction (conventionally indicated by a leading asterisk), it has known analogues in the other early Germanic languages (Old Norse *austr* and Old High German *ōstar*) and thus provides a coherent etymology for both the goddess and month names. Shaw notes that although the comparative name element *ēast(e)ra* meaning 'more east' could provide an alternative origin for the name *Eostre*, the use of <tur> and <tor> spellings in the earliest examples of *Eosturmonath* (see table 21) would tend to argue against this (Shaw 2011, 59–60).

Manuscript	Month Name 1	Month Name 2	Deity Name
Cologne, Dombibliothek, MS 83(ii), ff.104r–104v	*eosturmanath*	*eostormonath*	*eostre*
Cologne, Dombibliothek, MS 102, ff.30r–31r	*eosturmonath*	*eosturmonath*	*eosdre*
Cologne, Dombibliothek, MS 103, ff.80r–81r	*eosturmonath*	*eosturmonath*	*eostrae*
St Gallen, Stiftsbibliothek, MS 250, 216–218	*eusturmonath*	*eosturmonath*	*eostre*

Table 21. Spellings of *Eostre* and *Eosturmonath* transcribed from ninth-century manuscripts of Bede's *De Temporum Ratione*, from digital images available online at: www.ceec.uni-koeln.de and www.e-codices.unifr.ch/en.

The next class of evidence that Shaw considers is a small number of Old English (Anglo-Saxon) place names that are thought to contain the element *ēastor*, including Eastrington in East Yorkshire, Eastrea in Cambridgeshire and Eastry in Kent (see figure 9). The oldest surviving references to Eastrington (*Eastringatun*) and Eastrea (*Estrey*) are found in what purport to be mid tenth-century land charters, but are more likely to be eleventh- or twelfth-century forgeries (Sawyer 1968, charters 681 and 741). That being said, these documents still provide the earliest known record of the two place names, which both use a <tr> spelling (with no medial vowel) as do their modern equivalents. Thus, while these two spellings could in theory stem from the reconstructed element *ēastor*, they could just as likely derive from the comparative element *ēast(e)ra* (Shaw 2011, 58–60). Nevertheless, Shaw is more confident that *ēastor* forms the first element of Eastry in Kent, where two ninth-century charters provide examples of the place name with <tor> spellings (Brooks and Kelly 2013, charters 39 and 43) (see table 22). The second element of this place name is a rare example of the Old English *gē* meaning 'district' or 'region' and corresponds to the German *gau*, Dutch *gouw* and West Frisian *goa*. The word *gau* is found in various continental (Carolingian) documents where is is equated with the Latin word *pagus*, a term that was used by the Romans to describe early Celtic and Germanic sub-tribal groupings (Shaw 2011, 68).

No.	Sawyer	AD	Manuscript	Spelling	
24	128	788	Canterbury Dean and Chapter, Charter M 340, f.1r	*Eastrgena*	× 1
39	1500	805–832	British Library, Stowe Charter 8, f.1r	*Eastorege*	× 1
43	1264	811	British Library, Cotton MS Augustus II. 47, f.1r	*Easterege*	× 2
				Eosterege	× 1
				Eosterge	× 2
				Eostorege	× 2
62	1268	825–832	British Library, Cotton MS Augustus II. 72, f.1r	*Eastrœge*	× 1
140	914	1006	British Library, Cotton MS Claudius A. III, f.2r and f.4v (thought to be an eleventh-century forgery)	*Eastrige*	× 2

Table 22. Occurrences of Eastry in the Anglo-Saxon charters of Christ Church, Canterbury (Brooks and Kelly 2013), with spellings verified using published images (Sanders 1878, plate II; Sanders 1884, plate VIII) and digital images of the original manuscripts available online at www.bl.uk/manuscripts.

Evidence that some Anglo-Saxon personal names may have used the same first element was unwittingly recorded by Bede in his biography of *Eosteruini* or Easterwine (650–86 AD) the Abbot of Wearmouth (King 1930, 2: 407–15). Shaw identifies a further three occurrences of the name in the ninth-century *Durham Liber Vitae* (Rollason and Rollason 2007)—a Northumbrian confraternity book recording the names (and ranks) of the monks and nuns in early monasteries of north-east England—along with an abbess *Aestorhild*, whose name is believed to be the origin of the Middle English *Estrild*. The four examples found in the *Durham Liber Vitae* (see table 23) clearly use either <tor> or <tur> spellings in their second syllable, thus reinforcing the argument that *ēastor* forms the first element of these personal names (Shaw 2011, 60–61).

Folio	Monastic Rank	Name
16r	*Nomina reginarum et abbatissarum* (queen and abbess)	Aestorhild
20r	*Nomina abbatum* (abbot)	Aesturuini
26r	*Nomina diaconorum* (deacon)	Aeostoruini
28v	*Nomina clericorum* (cleric)	Eosturuini

Table 23. Personal names and monastic ranks transcribed from the ninth-century *Durham Liber Vitae* (London, British Library, Cotton MS Domitian A.VII, ff.15r–45r), from digital images available online at www.bl.uk/manuscripts.

In these Old English examples, that appear to use the same element for deity, locality and personal names, Shaw sees a parallel with the matron cults of the Lower Rhine:

> The name *Eostre* is, then, perhaps not unrelated to traditions of naming people and places. And we have seen such interlocking traditions of divine names with localities and personal names before—in the evidence for matron cults. (Shaw 2011, 61)

However, these Old English names, and Shaw's assessment of them, clearly deserve further consideration. Interestingly, Shaw does not explore the semantic relationship between *Eostre* and *Eosturmonath* in any detail, with just two brief references to 'her month' and 'the month connected with her name' (Shaw 2011, 69); and a related newspaper article in which he describes *Eostre* as 'a goddess whose name was attached to a month by the pagan Anglo-Saxons' (Shaw 2012). Nevertheless, these extracts clearly agree with of Bede's account that *Eosturmonath* 'was once called after a goddess of theirs named Eostre' (Wallis 1999, 54). Based on this explanation we might logically assume (regardless of the exact linguistic process) that the pre-existing goddess name was later 'connected' or 'attached' to this month of the year, resulting in what Bede understood to be a theophoric (deity derived) month name. Shaw notes that most of the early manuscripts contain spellings of the month name that more closely agree with **ēastor* (Shaw 2011, 59–60), the same element that he identifies in the names *Aeostoruini* and *Aestorhild* listed in the *Durham Liber Vitae* (Shaw 2011, 60–61). Similar to other Old English (and Germanic) personal names, these examples are dithematic and comprise two elements: the prototheme **ēastor* followed by the deuterothemes *wine* (friend or follower) and *hild* (battle). That being said, Shaw rejects the possibility that this could be theophoric prototheme referencing *Eostre*, claiming this to be 'unacceptable on linguistic grounds' because 'the name element is **ēastor* not the feminine form used for the goddess's name' (Shaw 2011, 60). However, this assertion results in a potential contradiction. In the earliest examples of the month and personal names we clearly see both <tor> and <tur> spellings being used in the second syllable, thus reinforcing the argument that their first element or prototheme is **ēastor*. Consequently, to claim that *Eostur-monath* (see table 21) can be interpreted as 'her month' or the month the goddess name was attached to, while rejecting any suggestion that *Eostur-uini* (see table 23) could imply a similar connection to *Eostre*, is at least inconsistent if not contradictory.

Thus we clearly have two competing interpretations of the personal name Easterwine, which can be understood as either 'Eastern-friend' or 'Eostre's-follower'. A useful way to assess these interpretations is by noting the presence or absence of comparable names in the *Onomasticon Anglo-Saxonicum* (Searle 1897) and the *Prosopography of Anglo-Saxon England* (PASE 2008). If the name meant 'Eastern-friend' then we might logically expect to find other Old English names using at least one of the remaining cardinal points (north, south or west) as their prototheme and *wine* as their deuterotheme, but we don't—excluding a continental monk named *Nordoinus* (Searle 1897, 359; Piper 1884, 251). Alternatively, if the name meant 'Eostre's-follower' then we might logically expect to find other Old English names using similar mythological or theophoric elements as their prototheme and *wine* as their shared deuterotheme, which we do—including *Ælfwine*, *Freawine*, *Ingwine* and *Oswine*. Recent work by Leonard Neidorf (2022) has investigated these and other related theophoric names, by closely examining the use and meaning of their prototatemes: *ælf* (elf), *frea* (lord) *Ing* (deity name) and *os* (god). The names *Ælfwine* and *Oswine* are well attested in Old English sources, and, like other dithematic names, remained in use long after the Anglo-Saxons converted to Christianity (Searle 1897, 27– 30 and 380– 381). The name *Freawine* is found in the royal genealogies of Wessex as a descendant of the god Woden and ancestor of Cerdic the first king of West Saxons (*Anglo-Saxon Chronicle*, 552 AD). Its prototheme is cognate with the Old Norse deity name *Freyr*, and the equivalent term *Freys vinr* (Frey's follower) is used in the *Poetic Edda* to describe the legendary hero Sigurd (*Sigurðarkviða in skamma*, stanza 24). The Old English deuterotheme *wine* is clearly cognate with the Old Norse term *vinr*, with the wider meanings of 'friend', 'follower' and 'worshipper'. Supporting evidence for this interpretation is found in the epic poem *Beowulf* where the besieged king Hrothgar is twice described as the *eodor/frean Ingwina* or 'lord of Ing's followers' (*Beowulf*, lines 1044 and 1319). Furthermore, in Old Norse mythology the god *Freyr* is equated with *Yngvi*, appearing in the compound names *Yngvi-Freyr* and *Ingunar-Freyr*, which are clearly cognate with the prototatemes in *Freawine* and *Ingwine* and perhaps suggest that these Old English names also had related meanings (Neidorf, 2021, 381-382). Interestingly, both *Freyr* (lord) and his sister *Freyja* (lady) were members of the *Vanir* group of gods and goddesses (associated with fertility), whose male and female deities appear to have been more active in the in the summer and winter half-years, respectively (Gunnell 2021, 244–245): 'The implication is that both parties must occasionally meet up, albeit briefly, at the turning of the seasons (or perhaps at their mid-points)' (Gunnell 2021, 245). Thus, it might be suggested that *Eostre*, who was celebrated around the spring equinox, served a similar function with the transition from the dark-winter to light-summer months. These examples would tend to support the 'Eostre's follower' interpretation of Easterwine, and clearly demonstrate that a theophoric interpretation cannot be ruled out.

Although the three place names examined by Shaw are widely believed to contain the first element *ēastor* (Ekwall 1960, 156–58), Eastrington and Eastrea are largely abandoned due to their ambiguous <tr> spellings, leaving Eastry in Kent as his main focus of attention. The village of Eastry (Ordnance Survey: TR310545) and its surrounding parish lie on the ancient road between the Roman forts of Richborough (*Rutupiae*) and Dover (*Dubris*). Two early Anglo-Saxon cemeteries have been located within the village, along with the site of an early royal manor or *ville* where King Egbert of Kent (664–73 AD) allegedly had his two young cousins Ethelred and Ethelbert put to death in 665 AD. Anglo-Saxon charter evidence (Brooks and Kelly 2013) and the later *Domesday Book* (1086 AD) would indicate that the village was once the centre of an early Kentish sub-kingdom, which went on to become one of the county's seven pre-Norman 'lathes' or administrative units (Lloyd 2013). The Lathe of Eastry survived until the thirteenth century when it was combined with the Lathe of Borough to form the new Lathe of St Augustine, while the much smaller Eastry Hundred survived until the late nineteenth century when its functions were largely superseded under the *Local Government*

Act (1894). The place name is generally interpreted as meaning the 'eastern district' or 'eastern region' (**ēastor* + *gē*), which clearly reflects its easternmost position in Kent. Its nearest English parallel is the county name Surrey meaning the 'southern district' or 'southern region' (*sūðer* + *gē*). However, there are a number of direct parallels on the European mainland, including *Ostergau* in Switzerland, *Oostergouw* in North Holland, and *Eastergoa* in West Friesland. Nevertheless, Shaw's treatment of the place-name evidence for Eastry is rather selective:

> The early forms of Eastry clearly show the presence of the vowel /o/ in the second syllable of *eastor*, demonstrating that this is unlikely to be an instance of *ēastra*: where *ēastra* is spelt with a vowel graph between the <t> and <r>, it is always <e>. (Shaw 2011, 59)

Shaw neglects to mention that in addition to the three examples of the place name with <tor> spellings, the early charters include another five examples with <ter> spellings, and four examples with the ambiguous <tr> spelling (see table 22). Moreover, two of the three examples with <tor> spellings appear in the same charter as the five examples with <ter> spellings (Brooks and Kelly 2013, charter 43). If we follow Shaw's line on thinking, these <tor> spellings are unlikely to represent the element *ēast(e)ra*, whereas the <ter> spellings could only represent this element. However, the appearance of these two different spellings in the very same charter must cast doubt on the significance being attached to them by Shaw, and whether they can be said to reveal which of the two place-name elements **ēastor* or *ēast(e)ra* was the original. Did the pre-literate early inhabitants of Eastry make any distinction between these two place-name elements, or did they (as perhaps indicated the charter evidence) use them interchangeably?

In a further attempt to connect the the cult of *Eostre* with Eastry in Kent, the initial <eo> diphthong found in almost half the early examples of the place name (see table 22) is likened to

Bede's spellings of *Eostre* and *Eosturmonath*, and suggested to have been an orthographic feature or linguistic trait that was more common in Kent than in Bede's home region of Northumbria (Shaw 2011, 64–65). In support of this argument, Shaw cites Bede's use of the same initial diphthong 'on occasion in the name of Eadbald of Kent (616-640 AD), probably reflecting the orthography of his source or sources' (Shaw 2011, 65). However, the suggestion that Bede's renderings of these names could 'reflect his use of a written source from outside his own locality' (Shaw 2011, 65), and more specifically from Kent, can be refuted using Shaw's own sources. Evidence of the initial <eo> diphthong being used in a local Northumbrian context is clearly provided by the personal names *Aeostoruini* and *Eosturuini* recorded in the *Durham Liber Vitae* (see table 23); while Bede's accounts of *Aeodbaldus* (King of Kent) and *Eosteruini* (Abbot of Wearmouth) reveal him using of the same initial diphthong in the names of historical figures from both Kent and Northumbria (King 1930, 1: 232, 238, 246, and 2: 407–15).

Shaw's suggestion that it was the influence of Canterbury within the early Anglo-Saxon church that enabled this local Kentish name to be adopted throughout England, and that Bede may have been relying a written source from Canterbury for his explanation of the month names, is simply speculation (Shaw 2011, 65). In his preface to the *Historia Ecclesiastica* Bede firstly acknowledges Abbot Albinus of Canterbury as his principal authority, along with Nothelm, who was then priest in London and later Bishop of Canterbury. From them he received information regarding the province of Kent and the Gregorian/Augustinian mission in particular. However, Bede also claims to have received information from Daniel the Bishop of Winchester regarding Wessex, Sussex and the Isle of Wight, the monks at Lastingham regarding Mercia and Essex, Abbot Esius of East Anglia and Cunebert the Bishop of Lindsey. Lastly, he credits the monks at Lindisfarne and innumerable other Northumbrian witnesses, which almost certainly included his own monastery at Jarrow-Monkwearmouth (King 1930, I, 4–9). It is therefore impossible say which, if any, of these sources may have provided Bede with his information on the origins of the English month names. And as mentioned earlier (in Chapter 3), it is equally likely that Bede's information did not come from any written source, but from the personal knowledge or recollections of the people he knew, including members of his own family, who perhaps 'could remember the heyday of Northumbrian heathenism' (Mayr-Harting 1991, 22).

While the evidence set out by Shaw appears to support his argument that the reconstructed element *ēastor was used in at least one Old English month name and a small number of personal names, the evidence for its use as a place-name element is more ambiguous. Disproportionate significance is attached to the choice of unstressed vowel in the second syllable of one Old English (Kentish) place-name—emphasising a minority of examples with <tor> (× 3) spellings over the majority with <tr> (× 4) and <ter> (× 5) spellings—and where the semantic values (meanings) of the two likely place-name elements (*ēastor 'eastern' and ēast(e)ra 'more east') are so close that they are practically synonyms, thus explaining the observed interchange between them. Moreover, the suggestion that the initial <eo> diphthong in Eostre and Eosturmonath could indicate Bede's use written sources from outside his home region, and from Kent in particular, is contradicted by its appearance in at least three Northumbrian personal names (recorded in the Durham Liber Vitae and Bede's Historia Abbatum), thereby disproving the philological case for Eostre having been a specifically Kentish goddess. Nevertheless, Shaw likens these 'interlocking [naming] traditions' to the matron cults of Germania Inferior, and suggests that Eostre was a local goddess whose development can be said to have paralleled that of the Matronae Austriahenae:

> It is not implausible to suggest that the names of Eostre and of the Austriahenae are etymologically similar, not because they are directly related to one another, but because they reflect similar

broad patterns of naming practices in the early Germanic languages. In other words, these are deities with local importance, whose names developed in parallel ways to refer to an area or group that was in some way identified as eastern. (Shaw 2011, 64)

A further deficiency in Shaw's argument, in that we have no evidence of any other Anglo-Saxon gods or goddesses with names based on the cardinal directions (north, south or west).

With regard to Eastry in Kent and a possible link with the cult of *Eostre*, Shaw focusses on the names of the adjacent pre-Norman administrative units and the collective names given to their inhabitants: the Lathe of Borough (Canterbury) was inhabited by the *Burhwara*, the Lathe of Lympne by the *Limenwara*, and the Lathe of Wye by the the *Wiwara* (Brooks 1989, 73; Lloyd 2013, 94). Shaw rightly points out that 'there is no direct evidence for a conception of the inhabitants of the region [Lathe] of Eastry as a distinct social grouping'; that being said, he thinks it likely that they would have been known as the *Eastorwara signifying the 'inhabitants of the eastern area' (Shaw 2011, 67). Expanding on this idea he suggests that:

> Such a local social grouping, below the level of kingdom or tribe, offers a plausible analogue for the groupings within which the cults of matrons evidently operated. None of this proves any specific connection between *Eostre* and Eastry, of course, but this does make a case for the existence in pre-Christian England of relatively small-scale social groupings which quite possibly had their own local, group-specific goddesses—and *Eostre* could well be just such a goddess. (Shaw 2011, 67)

To assess whether *Eostre* and the *Matronae Austriahenae* may be characterised as parallel or analogous developments, we should begin by asking whether the two cults have any common or shared attributes—a question that has been succinctly answered by the folklorist Stephen Winnick at the Library of Congress:

> The *Matronae Austriahenae* are triple goddesses for whom it was customary to leave votive inscriptions on stone, while *Eostre* is a single goddess to whom no inscription has ever been found, but whom it was customary to celebrate in April. In other words, these two goddess concepts have no known attributes in common, and therefore don't seem to be closely related. (Winnick 2016)

While Shaw does not suggest any direct relationship between the two cults, he does view them as parallel developments that reflect common naming practices among the early Germanic peoples; exhibiting three shared characteristics as: (a) group-specific local deities, (b) deriving their name from a small-scale social group or area, and (c) defined as 'eastern' with reference to other adjacent groups or areas.

However, apart from their cognate deity names and female gender, there is no evidence that the two goddess concepts shared any other attributes or characteristics. While the *Matronae Austriahenae* were certainly a very localised cult with a temple site likely to have existed in the Morken-Harff area, and a collective name that may have been used by some of their followers—the 'Austriates' (genitive *Austriatium*) found in one inscription (see table 20)—there is no proof that this term was derived to the local social geography or that it served as the local group or area name. Conversely, while the earliest examples of the place name Eastry point toward the presence of an 'eastern' region or district in Kent, whose inhabitants may have borne a related group name, there is no evidence to suggest that the cult of *Eostre* was specifically connected with Eastry or the surrounding part of Kent. What Shaw seems to be doing is taking the evidence from one cult or location, and then using this evidence to infer its existence in the other cult or location, and *vice versa*. However, this looks very similar to a kind reasoning that Shaw has consistently cautioned against (Shaw 2002; Shaw 2007):

> How similar any Anglo-Saxon cult of Woden was to the cult of Odin in Scandinavia is not an easy question to answer, and it is, I would suggest, a question that cannot simply be dismissed in favour of an assumption that Odin's characteristics must also have been Woden's characteristics, and *vice versa*... even if we accept that their names are linguistically cognate. (Shaw 2011, 12 and 15)

Nevertheless, there is perhaps an even more fundamental question that needs to be addressed, which is whether the *Matronae Austriahenae* were truly representative of wider Germanic deity-naming practices (outside the Roman empire), and thus whether they can be said provide a parallel for understanding the cult of *Eostre*? In order to answer this question we need to revisit some of the points raised in the previous chapter. If we take Shaw's (2012) 'matrons of the easterners' translation, and apply his 'matron names and localities' model (see table 19), we can justifiably argue that the *Austriahenae* was a pan-tribal or wider area name, where the dedicators were distant or removed from their ancestral home-land in the east—an interpretation that clearly accords with the history the local Ubian people. In recent research the *Austriahenae* epithet has been likened to those of other matron cults whose devotees are thought to have originated outside the province of Germania Inferior, while their shared suffix (*-henae*) is now thought indicate an originally Celtic word-formation process and deity-naming practice (De Bernardo Stempel 2019, 122–128 and 138–143). By the middle of the second century AD there had been almost two hundred years of Roman (Latin), Gallo-Belgic (Celtic) and Ubian (Germanic) interaction in the region, which would ac-count for the different linguistic influences observed in the various matron names. Shaw notes that these matron cults, with their Germanic and Celtic epithets, were concentrated in the area inhabited by the *Ubii*, and believes them to provide evidence of an indigenous ancestor cult that existed in this area before it came under Roman control (Shaw 2011, 42–43)—and thus before the *Ubii* were relocated there in 39 BC. However, it begs the question whether this native mother-goddess cult ever existed among the Germanic tribes living to the east of the Rhine, (including the premigration *Ubii*) or was reflective of their deity-naming traditions. Accordingly, this throws into doubt whether *Eostre* and the *Matronae Austriahenae* (in particular) can be claimed to provide evidence of parallel early Germanic deity-naming practices. Thus making it hard to support Shaw's forthright assertions that: (a) 'We have found evidence for parallel naming practices in an early Anglo-Saxon goddess and a group of matrons' and (b) 'Eostre appears to have been principally defined by her relationship to a social and geographical grouping' (Shaw 2011, 70 and 71).

Shaw dismisses the idea that *Eostre* was a 'functional' spring or dawn goddess, and denies the possibility that her cult was related to the dawn goddesses observed in other Indo-European cultures (Shaw 2011, 55 and 71):

> This... does away with the need to make special arguments for a relationship between the words related to 'east' and the idea of the dawn or even Spring. There is, in fact, little reason to suppose that the Germanic languages usually treated 'east' and its relatives and derivatives as related to dawn. Latin uses the word *oriens* to mean both 'east' and 'dawning' and terms like the Latin *aurora* ('dawn') are ultimately etymologically related to the word 'east' in the Germanic languages. This is, however, a very ancient connection... that pre-dates Proto-Germanic. (Shaw 2011, 64)

Justifiably, Shaw highlights the fact that Bede provides no information to connect *Eostre* with the dawn, and that, unlike some Indo-European languages (including Latin), Germanic words meaning 'east' are not synonyms for 'dawn'. That being said, the self-evident link between the east and the dawn would have been clearly apparent to the speakers of any early Germanic language, including Old English, as demonstrated by the following extract from the *Exeter Book* of Anglo-Saxon poetry: *oþþæt eastan cwom ofer deop-gelad dægred-woma* 'until from out the east there came o'er the deep way the rush of dawn' (Saint Guthlac, poem B, lines 1291-92; Gollancz 1895, 182–83). It may similarly be observed that Bede provides no information to suggest that *Eostre* was the local tutelary deity of an 'eastern' sub-tribal group or area. What Bede does tell us is that the goddess' celebrations occurred during *Eosturmonath*, a month that broadly corresponded to the Julian calendar month of April, which in the northern hemisphere placed her period veneration in the springtime of the year. Furthermore, as the fourth lunar month of the Anglo-Saxon year, which according to Bede commenced on the eighth *kalends* of January (25 December), *Eosturmonath* would generally have begun on or about the spring equinox.

The question that Shaw strangely fails to address, or even acknowledge, is why his local group-specific version of the goddess *Eostre* would have been worshipped at this specific time of year. Most modern linguists would hopefully agree that *Eosturmonath* represents a combination of two Old English elements collectively meaning either 'east-month' or 'eastern-month'. If that is the case, then the commencement of this lunar month near the spring equinox—when the sun and nearest full moon both rise in their more easterly positions on the horizon (subject to local topography)—supplies us with a simple and coherent rationale for both the timing and etymology of *Eosturmonath*. These annual solar and lunar events would have been clearly visible to the Germanic-speaking communities living on (and farming) the flat coastal lands around the southern half of the North Sea, which included the ancestral homelands of the Anglo-Saxons and the eastern seaboard of Britain where they first settled. Moreover, this full moon (nearest the spring equinox) would often have coincided with the Paschal full moon that was used to determine the Christian date of Easter, which clearly resonates with Bede's account that it was the coincidence of Christian and pagan celebrations in this month that prompted the renaming of the Paschal season and festival: 'calling the joys of the new rite by the time-honoured name of the old observance' (Wallis 1999, 54). The impetus for the Church's adoption of this native month name may also be seen in a letter sent by Pope Gregory the Great (in 601 AD) to his missionaries in England, in which he urged them to hold solemn feasts together on the days of the Christian holy martyrs, and to accept any offerings made by the pagan Anglo-Saxons 'to their devils' and to rededicate them in praise of 'the true God' (King 1930, 1: 163). That being said, the decision to rename of the Christian festival that celebrates the most theologically important events in the life of Christ (the Last Supper, Crucifixion, and Resurrection), is not a choice these clerics and missionaries would made lightly or without very good reason. This would suggest that the *Eosturmonath* celebrations were so deeply embedded in the culture of the pagan Anglo-Saxons 'that the adoption of the Old English name was a conscious and necessary decision to help win over converts to the new faith' (Sermon 2022, 153).

It may be observed that Bede offers similar astronomical and seasonal explanations for two of Anglo-Saxon month names. *Winterfilleth* (October) is said to derive its name from the first full moon of the old winter half-year (between autumn and spring equinoxes); and the twin months of *Guili* (December and January) to derive their name from the winter solstice when the sun 'turns back' and the hours of daylight slowly begin to increase:

> *Unde et mensem quo hyemalia tempora incipiebant Vuinterfylleth appellabant, composito nomine ab hyeme et plenilunio, quia videlicet a plenilunio ejusdem mensis hyems sortiretur initium... Menses Giuli a conversione solis in auctum diei, quia unus eorum praecedit, alius subsequitur, nomina accipiunt.* (Jones 1977, 330–31)

Hence they called the month in which the winter season began

Winterfilleth, a name made up from 'winter' and 'full Moon', because winter began on the full Moon of that month... The
months of *Giuli* derive their name from the day when the Sun
turns back [and begins] to increase, because one [of these
months] precedes [this day] and the other follows. (Wallis 1999,
54)

In the next chapter we will be looking at these astronomical and
calendrical relationships in more detail.

CHAPTER 11

Yeavering:

Edwin's 'Grandstand' or Eostre's Observatory?

With no supporting documentary evidence for the cult of *Eostre*, is there anything in the archaeological record we can consider? Richard North (2012) has identified a number of possible spring and near equinoctial sunrise alignments at Yeavering in Northumberland, the seventh-century Bernician seat of royal power, which he suggests may have been associated with the cult of *Eostre*. These alignments are said to have been marked by several free-standing wooden posts, east-west inhumation burials and timber building orientations. The most significant of which was first identified by the site's excavator, Brian Hope-Taylor (1977, 132, figure 63), as a principal east-west axis respected by at least seven major structures across the site, including its two great halls and a unique theatre or assembly structure (see table 24). Hope-Taylor believed that these structures had a 'metrological and axial relationship' and that they demonstrated a clear 'east-west axis of structural symmetry' in phases II and III of his site chronology (Hope-Taylor 1977, 141 and 202), which he dated to the reigns of Æthelfrith and Edwin (c. 605–632 AD). Hope-Taylor went on to discuss the free-standing posts' possible ritual, symbolic and totemic significance, but did not consider their potential astronomical or calendrical significance (Hope-Taylor 1977, 258–260).

Structure	Description
Post BX	Free-standing post with an adjacent east-west burial
Post AX	Free-standing post with an adjacent east-west burial
Building A4	Largest rectangular hall aligned east-west with axis through its end doors
Building A2	Second largest rectangular hall aligned east-west with axis through its end doors
Post E	Free-standing post at eastern apex of building E
Building E	Wedge-shaped structure interpreted as a theatre or assembly
Building D2	Rectangular hall aligned north-south with axis through its side doors

Table 24. Structures on Yeavering's principal east-west axis according to Hope-Taylor (1977).

North (2012) argues that during the early post-Roman period the native British at Yeavering worshipped a personification of the spring equinox by means of observational astronomy; a deity that may have been worshipped in the area since the Iron Age, given the majority of roundhouses found within the nearby hillfort on Yeavering Bell have broadly east-facing doorways. During the sixth century AD the Angles had settled along the coastal areas of Bernicia and Deira (later united to form the kingdom of Northumbria), and progressively extended their power and influence inland towards the west. In the following century they gained control over further British territory and populations in the Pennines, including the Cheviot Hills and the site at Yeavering. North suggests that during this period of Anglo-British interaction the Anglian kings of Bernicia adopted the former British seat of power at Yeavering, along with its local equinoctial deity. The site's principal east-west axis (identified by Hope-Taylor) and its easterly sunrise alignment (identified by North) is therefore interpreted as a physical expression and manifestation of the deity, which in translation became the Anglian goddess *Eostre*. Bede records that sometime after king Edwin was converted to Christianity by

Paulinus in 627 AD he invited the bishop to his royal seat at Yeavering (*Adgefrin*), where over a period 36 days Paulinus preached to the local population and baptised them in the nearby river Glen (King 1930, 1, 290–291). North suggests that this event took place during the Paschal season, which coincided with the local celebrations of *Eostre*. He goes on to propose that it was Paulinus, in response to Pope Gregory's doctrine of inculturation, who first applied the name of this local pagan deity to the Christian Paschal season, which then spread to the rest of England through its wider adoption and use in the Anglo-Saxon church.

North's ideas are very interesting, given Yeavering's role as an early Northumbrian royal centre and its proximity to Bede's monastery at Jarrow (see figure 9). However, there are a number of problems with his native British goddess theory. Firstly, there is no evidence of any British to Anglian ritual (or settlement) continuity at Yeavering. While the incoming Anglo-Saxons were pagan and often reused prehistoric ritual or funerary monuments as a focus for their own burials, this reuse of much earlier Neolithic and Bronze Age monuments (including those at Yeavering) does not represent ritual continuity. Furthermore, the north-east to south-east facing doorways of the roundhouses on Yeavering Bell may simply reflect a pragmatic response to avoid the prevailing wind, particularly on such an exposed hilltop, and is typical of Iron Age roundhouses both regionally and nationally (Oswald and Pearson 2005, 115). Secondly, the historical works of Gildas, Bede and Nennius, along with the Old Welsh poems found in the *Llyfr Aneirin* and *Llyfr Taliesin*, including the epic poem *Y Gododdin*, all suggest that the post-Roman Britons of the *Hen Ogledd* (Old North) were largely Christian. Supporting evidence for this is found in the *Life of St Wilfrid* when describing various lands in the Pennines that had been granted to him by the Northumbrian kings, 'which the British clergy had deserted when fleeing from the hostile sword wielded by the warriors of our own nation' (Colgrave 1927, 36–37). Thirdly, we have no evidence that Paulinus' visit to Yeavering was at Easter, only that it occurred sometime after King Edwin's conversion in 627 AD. Following Edwin's death at the battle of Hatfield Chase in 632 or 633 AD his kingdom quickly reverted back to paganism, which saw his queen, young children and bishop Paulinus, flee south to the Christian kingdom of Kent.

Nevertheless, North's astronomical alignments do warrant further consideration, the principal ones relating to the unique and enigmatic structure E, variously interpreted as a theatre, grandstand or assembly (Hope-Taylor 1977, 119–122 and 124). The structure was focused on post E, which formed the apex of this wedge-shaped or trapezoidal building (as viewed from above), consisting of nine concentric arcs or crescent shape trenches of increasing length the further west they were positioned of post E. Each of these trenches contained the 'ghosts' of their timber foundations, in the form of post holes and linear slots that more accurately defined the nine arcs of the structure. Hope-Taylor suggested that these elements had been laid out by attaching a rope to post E and tracing each of the nine arcs on the ground at distances ranging from 17 to 68 feet, with a chord between the end points of the final arc measuring a little over 62 feet. Hope-Taylor interpreted these features as foundation elements supporting connected tiers of raised seating, for an assembly or grandstand, that were focused on post E and a central throne area (Hope-Taylor 1977, 121, figure 57). He compared the Yeavering structure to a segment of a Roman theatre or amphitheatre, which he suggested the Bernician kings were attempting to emulate and gain prestige from (Hope-Taylor 1977, 241–244). While this is still the generally accepted interpretation (Barnwell 2005), it has not gone without challenge:

> What is less convincing is the supposed theatre: the reconstruction has become a fact. Yet it has no obvious parallels, and that a segment of a circle could be thought of in the same terms

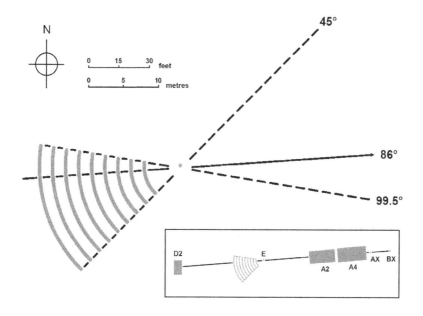

Figure 10. Plan of Yeavering's structure E, showing the free-standing post and nine arcs of the timber foundations in grey, and three sunrise alignments in black (drawn by the author).

as a semi-circular theatre or a completely circular amphitheatre is unconvincing. (Wood 2005, 188)

The principal sunrise alignments proposed by North are: (a) along the northern edge of structure E with an alignment in early March 'near enough to the start of Hredmonath', (b) between the posts E, AX and BX with an equinoctial alignment in late March 'before the start of Eosturmonath', and (c) along the southern edge of structure E with an alignment in early June at 'the end of Thrimil-chi' (North 2012, 17–18). However, in order to assess these possible alignments we first need to correct a fundamental mis-reading of the original site survey and structure E orientations. North's assumption that site's principal axis (E-AX-BX) 'runs nearly perfectly west-east' at azimuth of 90 degrees (North 2012, 6) is based on Hope-Taylor's geometrical illustration of Yeavering (Hope-Taylor 1977, 132, figure 63), where he uses this line as the horizontal axis for his drawing. However, the original site survey drawing and phase plans reveal that its true azimuth is closer to 86 degrees (Hope Taylor 1977, 46–47, 159–160, 162, figures 12 and 75–77). Therefore, by applying a simple correction of −4.0 degrees, the true azimuths of the E-North-Side and E-AX-BX alignments can be obtained. However, in order to correct the E-South-Side azimuth we need to apply a further correction of −3.0 degrees, which is the difference between North's assumed apex angle (51.5 degrees) and that recorded by Hope-Taylor:

> Its most conspicuous remains consisted of nine foundation-trenches describing concentric arcs of circles between two radii forming an angle of approximately 54° 30'. These trenches are numbered from 1 to 9, proceeding outwards from the centre-point (i.e., from what must be regarded as the front of the structure, to the back). (Hope-Taylor 1977, 199)

The corrected azimuths (see table 25 and figure 10) are all confirmed by Hope-Taylor's detailed plan of structure E, which shows not only the extent of the construction trenches, but also the more precise locations and orientations of its timber foundations (Hope-Taylor 1977, 120, figure 55). Further compounding these errors, North increases his alignments' altitudes to 2.5 degrees 'in order to take some account of Yeavering's 134-foot [correction 234-foot] elevation above sea-level, as well as the inner rampart of the Great Enclosure and the high ground some distance to the east between Yeavering and the coast' (North 2012, 16). He goes on to suggests that 'the Great Enclosure, with its high inner palisade, may have enabled a distant artificial horizon for some of these posited observations from Theatre E by Post E' (North 2012, 19). However, recent excavations at Yeavering (Semple 2024; Ralston and Miket 2024) have demonstrated that, while the site's timber buildings all appear to be Anglo-Saxon and date from the late sixth to the mid-seventh century AD (with carbon dates between 570–650 AD), Hope-Taylor's 'great cattle enclosure' (to the east of the settlement) was in fact a late Bronze Age to Iron Age hillfort (with carbon dates between 1000–100 BC). This enclosure ditch and rampart had long been filled in and levelled by the time the great hall (A4) was constructed, and thus could not have provided an artificial (elevated) horizon for any solar observations from structure E. While North suggests that the assembly structure's three sunrise alignments could have been used as markers for particular months in the Anglo-Saxon year, this fails to recognise that as lunar months their positions (relative to the solar calendar) would have moved each year, and thus could not be marked or indicated by a single solar azimuth. Nevertheless, the basic ideas outlined in North's paper are both original and plausible. The E-AX-BX sunrise alignment could have marked a near equinoctial date in the solar year that was significant to the early seventh century inhabitants of Yeavering; and such a date could have been related to the cult of *Eostre* and used to regulate the timing of her month (*Eosturmonath*) and celebrations. Likewise, post E and structure E could have served as the upright 'gnomon' and tiered 'dial' of a sunrise sundial, being used to observe and record specific dates and cut-off points in the solar year. Interestingly, Hope-Taylor shows the E-AX-BX axis running along the southern edge of post E, which makes perfect sense if using the (more precise) edge of the shadow to chart the sun's progress along the local horizon, rather than estimating mid-line of the shadow. In addition to which, the southern edge of post E provides a better centre (apex) for the nine arcs of the of the structure.

Alignment	North	Error	Correction	Hope-Taylor (figure 55)
E-North-Side	103.5	+4.0	103.5 – 4.0	99.5
E-AX-BX	90.0	+4.0	90.0 – 4.0	86.0
E-South-Side	52.0	+7.0	52.0 – 4.0 – 3.0	45.0

Table 25. Corrected azimuths for the Yeavering structure E and the posts E, AX and BX sunrise alignments.

In Bede's description of the English year and its lunar months (*monað* from *mona* meaning 'moon') he provides little astronomical detail, but does explain that the two months of *Guili* preceded and followed the winter solstice, which implies that the opposite two months of *Litha* similarly preceded and followed the summer solstice. Bede also explains that the English year was originally divided into just two seasons, with six summer months when the days are longer than the nights, and six winter months beginning with *Winterfilleth*, so named because winter began on the full moon of that month. So, what could an 'eastern-month' be referring to at the opposite time of year? Based on the information provided by Bede we can at least infer that *Eosturmonath* was: (a) the opposite lunar month to *Winterfilleth*, (b) the first of the six summer months with longer daylight hours, and (c) the month with its full moon marking the beginning of the summer half-year. Bede also records that it was the fourth lunar month (one lunation spanning 29.53 days) of the Anglo-Saxon year, which began on the eighth kalends of January (25 December). Thus, *Eosturmonath* would have commenced on or around the spring equinox, when the sun generally rises (subject to local topography) in its more easterly position on the horizon at an azimuth of around 90 degrees. The progress towards this event is more pronounced in northern Europe than it is in the southern latitudes of the ancient world, due to the axial tilt of the earth relative to its orbital plane around the sun (the obliquity of the ecliptic, 23.62 degrees in AD 600). Between its two extremes at the summer and winter solstices, the angular distance covered by the position (azimuth) of the rising sun as it progresses across the local horizon in Northumberland, is almost double what it is at the Equator (see table 26). A full moon occurs when the sun and the moon are in opposition (on opposite sides of the earth) and their ecliptic longitudes differ by 180 degrees. At the solstices this results in the sunrise and nearest full-moonrise occurring at their opposite extremes on the local horizon (see table 27). As we move away from the solstices the angular distance between the sunrise and full-moonrise progressively decreases, until their azimuths crossover at the equinox, with their angular distance then increasing towards the next solstice. The significance of these crossover events is now being more actively investigated by archaeologists (Silva and Pimenta 2012; Silva 216), and clearly has implications for our understanding of *Eostre* and the *Eosturmonath* full moon.

Location	Latitude	Declination	Sunrise Azimuth	Angular Distance
Arctic Circle	66.38	± 23.62	00.00 ↔ 180.00	180.00
Lindisfarne	55.68	± 23.62	44.71 ↔ 135.29	90.57
Yeavering	55.57	± 23.62	44.87 ↔ 135.13	90.25
Jarrow	54.98	± 23.62	45.72 ↔ 134.28	88.57
Rome	41.90	± 23.62	57.43 ↔ 122.57	65.14
Athens	37.97	± 23.62	59.45 ↔ 120.55	61.09
Varanasi	25.32	± 23.62	63.69 ↔ 116.31	52.62
Angkor Wat	13.41	± 23.62	65.68 ↔ 114.32	48.65
Equator	0.00	± 23.62	66.38 ↔ 113.62	47.24
Formula: cos(Az) = (sin(Dec) − sin(Lat) × sin(Alt)) / (cos(Lat) × cos(Alt))				

Table 26. Sunrise azimuth (range) and angular distances at different

locations and latitudes in the early seventh century AD (assuming a level horizon with an altitude of zero degrees and ignoring atmospheric refraction).

Event	Sunrise	Nearest Full Moonrise
Winter Solstice	Southeast	Northeast
Spring Equinox	East	East
Summer Solstice	Northeast	Southeast
Autumn Equinox	East	East

Table 27. Relative sunrise and nearest full-moonrise positions on the local horizon at the solstices and equinoxes.

Lunar calendars tend to have alternate month lengths of 29 and 30 days, which over a period twelve lunar months (354 days) fall short of the solar year by about eleven days. Thus, traditional lunisolar calendars (like the Jewish calendar) will insert an extra intercalary month every two to three years in order to correct this deficit, but may use different times of year and methods of calculating when to insert the additional month. Nevertheless, they all tend to result in a nineteen-year pattern of twelve common (twelve-month) and seven embolismic (thirteen-month) lunar years known as the Metonic cycle after Meton of Athens in the fifth century BC. At the beginning and end of this nineteen-year cycle the full moon will appear on the same solar calendar dates (taking account of leap years):

Metonic Cycle: CCE–CCE–CE–CCE–CCE–CCE–CE

(12 common years × 12 lunar months) + (7 embolismic years × 13 lunar months) = 235 lunar months × 29.53 days = 6939.55 days

19 mean solar years × 365.24 days = 6939.56 days

148

Much has been written on the origins of Bede's Old English month names, and whether his explanations were simply speculation, but less on how the early Anglo-Saxon calendar may actually have functioned. In order to reconstruct this calendar we need to make full use of the information provided by Bede (Jones 1977, 330–331; Wallis 1999, 54), and fill in the gaps with reasonable assumptions. Bede describes how each month followed the course of the moon through one lunation or cycle of moon phases, from which we may assume that, like other lunisolar calendars, they had alternate lengths of 29 and 30 days, with an average length of 29.5 days. Bede makes a comparison with the Hebrew (Jewish) calendar, which has its lunar months beginning at the new moon. Furthermore, his description of *Winterfilleth* and 'the full moon of that month' would imply the full moon occurred during the course of the month, which would again support the idea that the Anglo-Saxon months commenced at the new moon. The year began at the winter solstice and was flanked by two months named *Giuli* 'when the sun turns back to increase', which would suggest that the two months named *Litha* were similarly intended to precede and follow the summer solstice. However, these lunar months would have progressively fallen out of step with the solstices, by approximately eleven days each year. In order to correct the accumulated shortfall between the previous lunar and solar years a third (intercalary) month named *Litha* would occasionally be added to the summer season, and hence these embolismic lunar years were called *Thrilithi* (three Lithas). Nevertheless, this still leaves us with two important questions to answer: (a) what event signalled that it was an embolismic year requiring an additional intercalary month, and (b) how could this event be predicted to allow farming communities to plan their agricultural and ritual year? It seems doubtful they would have waited until the second month of *Litha* had occurred entirely (all 29 or 30 days) in advance of the summer solstice, and more likely that they would have sought to avoid that month's full moon (in the middle of the month) preceding this auspicious mid-point in the year. In order to predict this event, rather than waiting until the summer solstice each year, it would have been necessary to use an earlier cut-off point or points in the preceding months or year, and then monitor where the full moons fell in relation to these points. The spring equinox would have provided an ideal time at which to make this prediction, with the crossover of the sunrise and full-moonrise on the eastern horizon, and with their relative dates and positions it being possible to determine whether it was a common or embolismic lunar year.

While Yeavering's structure E could perhaps have functioned as an assembly building or moot, it appears to be over-engineered for this purpose and has no real archaeological parallel. The structure (and wider settlement) are located on a sand and gravel terrace above the River Glen at a height of 70 metres above sea level, with an open eastern aspect looking towards points on the local horizon (from Northmoor to Doddington Moor and Weetwood Moor) some 8.5 kilometres away, with an average height of 150 metres above sea level. Sunrise observations could thus have been made in reverse with the post (gnomon) casting its shadow over the arcs (or steps) of the assembly structure like a sundial. The declinations of the three possible sunrise alignments can now be calculated using their correct azimuths (bearings) and shared altitude (elevation) of 0.5 degrees, which is largely cancelled out by atmospheric refraction, with negligible solar parallax (see table 28). The azimuth and declination of the E-South-Side alignment is particularly interesting, given that at this latitude they are broadly consistent with the sunrise on or after the summer solstice. If we accept this to be original target of that alignment, we can then establish the nearest ordinal day numbers (from the first day after winter solstice) and corresponding declinations for the other sunrise alignments, taking account of the earth's elliptical orbit around the sun (see table 29).

Alignment	Latitude	Azimuth	Altitude	Parallax	Refraction	Declination
E-North-Side	55.567	99.500	0.500	0.002	0.483	-5.339
E-AX-BX	55.567	86.000	0.500	0.002	0.483	2.276
E-South-Side	55.567	45.000	0.500	0.002	0.483	23.584
Formula: sin(Dec) = sin(Lat) × sin(Alt + Par – Ref) + cos(Lat) × cos(Alt + Par – Ref) × cos(Az)						

Table 28. Calculated solar declinations of the structure E sunrise alignments, using their correct azimuths and altitude.

Alignment	Ordinal Day	Obliquity	Solar Year	Eccentricity	Perihelion	Declination
E-North-Side	76	23.620	365.240	0.017	63.000	-5.701
E-North-Side	77	23.620	365.240	0.017	64.000	-5.310
E-North-Side	78	23.620	365.240	0.017	65.000	-4.917
E-AX-BX	95	23.620	365.240	0.017	82.000	1.831
E-AX-BX	96	23.620	365.240	0.017	83.000	2.227
E-AX-BX	97	23.620	365.240	0.017	84.000	2.622
E-South-Side	183	23.620	365.240	0.017	170.000	23.620
E-South-Side	184	23.620	365.240	0.017	171.000	23.618
E-South-Side	185	23.620	365.240	0.017	172.000	23.609
Formulae: n = ordinal day number (OD) since the winter solstice; $n - 1$ = number of fractional days (from zero) since the winter solstice; $n - 13$ = number of fractional days since the Earth's perihelion; sin(Dec) = sin(-23.62) × cos(360/365.24 × ($n - 1$) + 360/π × 0.017 × sin(360/365.24 × ($n - 13$)))						

Table 29. Possible range of ordinal days (since the winter solstice) and calculated declinations for the structure E sunrise alignments (using early seventh century values for the Earth's obliquity of the ecliptic, orbital eccentricity and perihelion).

Alignment	Declination	Latitude	Altitude	Parallax	Refraction	Azimuth
E-North-Side	-5.310	55.567	0.500	0.002	0.483	99.447
E-AX-BX	2.227	55.567	0.500	0.002	0.483	86.087
E-South-Side	23.618	55.567	0.500	0.002	0.483	44.924
Formula: cos(Az) = (sin(Dec) – sin(Lat) × sin(Alt + Par – Ref)) / (cos(Lat) × cos(Alt + Par – Ref))						

Table 30. Calculated azimuths for structure E sunrise alignments, using their calculated declinations (from table 29) and correct altitude.

Based on this analysis, and by comparing the declinations in tables 28 and 29 (final columns), it would appear that ordinal days 77, 96 and 184 were the most likely observation dates for the structure E sunrise alignments. These ordinal day numbers and their calculated solar declinations can now be tested in a reverse calculation to see how closely their calculated azimuths (see table 30, final column) match the actual sunrise alignments at Yeavering (see table 28, third column). Interestingly, the intervals between these sunrise alignments are divisible into whole lunar months. While the interval between the E-North-Side and E-South-Side alignments (107 days) is not immediately divisible into whole lunar months, if we move forward another solar year (107 + 365 = 472 days), the interval is exactly divisible into sixteen (alternate 29 and 30 day) lunar months. Likewise, the interval between the E-North-Side and E-AX-BX alignments (19 days) is not immediately obvious, but if we again move forward another solar year (19 + 365 = 384 days), the interval is exactly divisible into thirteen lunar months. The interval between the E-AX-BX and E-South-Side alignments (88 days) is equivalent to the difference between the other two intervals (472 − 384 = 88 days), and is exactly divisible into three lunar months. The full sequence being:

E-N-S [+30+29+30+29+30+29+30+29+30+29

+30+29+30] E-AX-BX [+29+30+29] E-S-S

While these sunrise alignments could easily have been used to record specific dates or months in the solar year, they could not, by themselves, have been used to record specific dates or months in the Anglo-Saxon lunar year, for the reasons already outlined above. Nevertheless, by closely monitoring the (locally apparent) full moons from early March to late June, and then recording the following sunrise azimuths, Yeavering's structure E could have functioned as a lunisolar observatory; using its fixed ordinal days and sunrise alignments as cutoff points (see table 31), in order to predict the occurrence of future full moons and anticipate embolismic lunar years requiring an additional intercalary month.

Full Moon Cutoff (Julian Dates)			Sunrise Alignment (Julian Dates)			
ODI	Normal Year	Leap Year	OD2	Normal Year	Leap Year	Azimuth
76	Mar 4	Mar 3	77	Mar 5	Mar 4	99.4 ± 0.3
95	Mar 23	Mar 22	96	Mar 24	Mar 23	86.1 ± 0.3
183	Jun 19	Jun 18	184	Jun 20	Jun 19	44.9
Full Moon Cutoff (Gregorian Dates)			Sunrise Alignment (Gregorian Dates)			
ODI	Normal Year	Leap Year	OD2	Normal Year	Leap Year	Azimuth
76	Mar 7	Mar 6	77	Mar 8	Mar 7	99.4 ± 0.3
95	Mar 26	Mar 25	96	Mar 27	Mar 26	86.1 ± 0.3
183	Jun 22	Jun 21	184	Jun 23	Jun 22	44.9

Table 31. Ordinal day numbers with their lunar (OD1) and solar (OD2) observation dates in the early seventh-century Julian and proleptic Gregorian calendars.

Year AD	Full Moon on/after Ordinal Day 76			Full Moon on/after Ordinal Day 95			Full Moon on/after Ordinal Day 183		
	Julian Date	OD1	19 Day Range [76 to 94]	Julian Date	OD1	11 Day Range [95 to 105]	Julian Date	OD1	11 Day Range [183 to 193]
609	Mar 26	98	Outside	Mar 26	98	Inside	Jun 23	187	Inside
610	Mar 15	87	Inside	Apr 14	117	Outside	Jul 11	205	Outside
611	Mar 4	76	Inside	Apr 3	106	Outside	Jun 30	194	Outside
612	Mar 22	95	Outside	Mar 22	95	Inside	Jun 19	184	Inside
613	Mar 12	84	Inside	Apr 10	113	Outside	Jul 7	201	Outside
614	Mar 31	103	Outside	Mar 31	103	Inside	Jun 27	191	Inside
615	Mar 21	93	Inside	Apr 19	122	Outside	Jul 16	210	Outside
616	Mar 9	82	Inside	Apr 7	111	Outside	Jul 5	200	Outside
617	Mar 28	100	Outside	Mar 28	100	Inside	Jun 24	188	Inside
618	Mar 17	89	Inside	Apr 15	118	Outside	Jul 13	207	Outside
619	Mar 6	78	Inside	Apr 4	107	Outside	Jul 2	196	Outside
620	Mar 24	97	Outside	Mar 24	97	Inside	Jun 20	185	Inside
621	Mar 13	85	Inside	Apr 12	115	Outside	Jul 9	203	Outside
622	Apr 1	104	Outside	Apr 1	104	Inside	Jun 28	192	Inside
623	Mar 22	94	Inside	Apr 20	123	Outside	Jul 17	211	Outside
624	Mar 10	83	Inside	Apr 9	113	Outside	Jul 6	201	Outside
625	Mar 29	101	Outside	Mar 29	101	Inside	Jun 26	190	Inside
626	Mar 18	90	Inside	Apr 17	120	Outside	Jul 15	209	Outside
627	Mar 7	79	Inside	Apr 6	109	Outside	Jul 4	198	Outside
628	Mar 25	98	Outside	Mar 25	98	Inside	Jun 22	187	Inside

Table 32. Early seventh-century Julian calendar dates for full moons on or after ordinal day numbers 76, 95 and 183 (Walker 1997; Ahmed 2001).

To demonstrate how this might have worked we need to examine a series of early seventh-century full moon dates occurring on

or after ordinal days 76, 95 and 183, with the chosen sample covering the nineteen-year period leading up to Paulinus visit to
Yeavering in 627 AD (see table 32). These full moon dates and
ordinal day numbers demonstrate an inverse relationship where:
(a) if a full moon occurs 'inside' the first nineteen days of (and
including) ordinal day 76, then full moons will occur 'outside' the
first eleven days of (and including) ordinal days 95 and 183, and
conversely, (b) if a full moon occurs 'outside' the first nineteen
days of (and including) ordinal day 76, then full moons will occur
'inside' the first eleven days of (and including) ordinal days 95 and
183. In order to explain this relationship we need to understand
that these figures represent two important lunisolar intervals. The
nineteen-day interval is equivalent to the difference between one
embolismic (thirteen-month) lunar year and one solar year ($13 \times
29.53 - 365.24 = 18.65$ days), while the eleven-day interval is
equivalent to the shortfall between one common (twelve-month)
lunar year and one solar year ($12 \times 29.53 - 365.24 = -10.88$ days).
In other words, an embolismic thirteen-month lunar year will be
approximately nineteen days longer than the average solar year,
while a common twelve-month lunar year will be approximately
eleven days shorter than the average solar year. Therefore, if full
moons occur within the first eleven days of (and including) ordinal
days 95 and 183, in twelve lunar month's time (one common lunar
year) the corresponding full moons will occur before ordinal days
95 and 183; whereas, in thirteen-month lunar month's time (one
embolismic lunar year) the corresponding full moons will still occur on or after ordinal days 95 and 183. These lunisolar
relationships, and the structure E sunrise alignments, enable the
formulation of two simple calendrical and astronomical rules, that
in any given year:

> If a spring (March to April) full moon occurs between ordinal
> days 76 and 94 (inclusive) then it is a common (twelve-month)
> lunar year; conversely, if a full moon does not occur within this
> interval then it is an embolismic (thirteen-month) lunar year.

If a spring full moon is followed by a sunrise azimuth of between 99.7° and 86.5° (inclusive) then it is a common (twelve-month) lunar year; conversely, if a full moon does not occur within these parameters then it is an embolismic (thirteen-month) lunar year.

When these rules are applied to the full moon dates nearest the spring equinox (on or after ordinal day 76) they provide a reliable method for: (a) predicting the dates of future full moons (and new moons), and thereby regulating the lunars months of the Anglo-Saxon year, (b) determining common and embolismic (*Thrilithi*) lunar years, and when to insert the intercalary third month of *Litha*, and (c) ensuring that the full moon in the second month of *Litha* always occurs on or after the summer solstice (ordinal day 183).

Year AD	Solar Year	Full Moon Observation			Following Sunrise Azimuth				Lunar Year
		Julian Date	OD1	Range [76 to 94]	OD2	Azimuth		Range [99.7 to 86.5]	
609	N	Mar 26	98	Outside	99	83.9	84.0	Outside	E
610	N	Mar 15	87	Inside	88	91.6	91.7	Inside	C
611	N	Mar 4	76	Inside	77	99.4	99.4	Inside	C
612	L	Mar 22	95	Outside	96	86.4	86.1	Outside	E
613	N	Mar 12	84	Inside	85	93.5	93.8	Inside	C
614	N	Mar 31	103	Outside	104	80.6	80.5	Outside	E
615	N	Mar 21	93	Inside	94	87.6	87.5	Inside	C
616	L	Mar 9	82	Inside	83	95.4	95.2	Inside	C
617	N	Mar 28	100	Outside	101	82.5	82.6	Outside	E
618	N	Mar 17	89	Inside	90	90.2	90.3	Inside	C
619	N	Mar 6	78	Inside	79	98.0	98.0	Inside	C
620	L	Mar 24	97	Outside	98	85.0	84.7	Outside	E
621	N	Mar 13	85	Inside	86	92.8	93.1	Inside	C
622	N	Apr 1	104	Outside	105	79.9	79.8	Outside	E
623	N	Mar 22	94	Inside	95	86.9	86.8	Inside	C
624	L	Mar 10	83	Inside	84	94.7	94.5	Inside	C
625	N	Mar 29	101	Outside	102	81.7	81.9	Outside	E
626	N	Mar 18	90	Inside	91	89.5	89.6	Inside	C
627	N	Mar 7	79	Inside	80	97.3	97.3	Inside	C
628	L	Mar 25	98	Outside	99	84.3	84.0	Outside	E

Azimuths: column 1 figures obtained using *Moon Calculator* 6.0 (Ahmed 2001); column 2 figures calculated from their ordinal day numbers (OD2) using formulae in tables 29 and 30.

Table 33. Application of calendrical (OD1) and astronomical (OD2) rules to the full moons nearest the spring equinox (on or after ordinal day 76).

These results (see tables 32 and 33) hint at further ways in which structure E could have been organised and operated. The angular distance between each sunrise (azimuth), as it progresses along the local horizon, is much greater at the equinoxes than it is at the solstices; making it easier to record the occurrence of a full moon in relation to the following day's sunrise azimuth—by physically marking the sun's position (from its shadow) on the face of the tiered structure. However, if this first full moon or following sunrise were not visible, it would have been possible, by applying the same principles, to use one of the subsequent full moons and sunrise azimuths. This provides us with a means of further subdividing the face or 'dial' of structure E, by extending the observed pattern of full moon cutoff dates and following sunrise azimuths (see table 34). In combination with these radial divisions, the nine concentric arcs or eight steps (tiers) of the structure E, could have been used to record the occurrence of full moons and lunation patterns in previous years. The nineteen-year Metonic cycle, irrespective of the starting point, can be divided into a two closely matching sets of eight years or Octaeterides (a significant periodicity in lunisolar calendrics after which a new or full moon occurs on same day of the year plus one or two days) and a remaining set of three years (that may match the beginning or end of the two longer sets). The cycle of lunar years explored in this chapter conforms to the sequence: ECC-EC-ECC then ECC-EC-ECC and ECC, which could easily have been recorded on the eight concentric steps of structure E, and clearly demonstrates both the Octaeterides and the more accurate Metonic cycle (see table 35).

Radial Lines	N-Side	R-2	R-3	R-4	R-5	R-6	R-7	S-Side
Full Moon Cutoff (OD1)	76	95	106	124	135	154	165	183
Ordinal Day Increments	+19	+11	+18	+11	+19	+11	+18	
Sunrise Azimuth (OD2)	99.4	86.1	78.5	66.7	60.1	50.9	47.2	44.9
Azimuths: calculated from their ordinal day numbers (OD2) using formulae in tables 29 and 30.								

Table 34. Suggested radial 'dial' divisions of structure E, extending the observed pattern of full moon cutoff dates (OD1) and following sunrise azimuths (OD2).

Concentric Steps	Step 1	Step 2	Step 3	Step 4	Step 5	Step 6	Step 7	Step 8
Octaeterides and Metonic Cycle	E (1) E (9) E (17)	C (2) C (10) C (18)	C (3) C (11) C (19)	E (4) E (12) E (1)	C (5) C (13)	E (6) E (14)	C (7) C (15)	C (8) C (16)
Years AD	609 617 625	610 618 626	611 619 627	612 620 628	613 621	614 622	615 623	616 624
Full Moon Ordinal Days (OD1)	98 100 101	87 89 90	76 78 79	95 97 98	84 85	103 104	93 94	82 83
Full Moon Julian Dates (OD1)	Mar 26 Mar 28 Mar 29	Mar 15 Mar 17 Mar 18	Mar 4 Mar 6 Mar 7	Mar 22 Mar 24 Mar 25	Mar 12 Mar 13	Mar 31 Apr 1	Mar 21 Mar 22	Mar 9 Mar 10
Following Sunrise Azimuths (OD2)	84.0 82.6 81.9	91.7 90.3 89.6	99.4 98.0 97.3	86.1 84.7 84.0	93.8 93.1	80.5 79.8	87.5 86.8	95.2 94.5
Azimuths: calculated from their ordinal day numbers (OD2) using formulae in tables 29 and 30.								

Table 35. Suggested concentric 'dial' divisions of structure E, using data from table 33 to demonstrate the Octaeterides (eight lunar-year pattern) and Metonic cycle (nineteen lunar-year pattern).

In this chapter we have seen how Yeavering's unique and enigmatic structure E could, theoretically, have functioned as a sunrise observatory, and have been used to regulate the lunar months and years of the Anglo-Saxon calendar described by Bede. Similar solar horizon (sunrise and sunset) observatories with calendrical alignments are not unknown, have been proposed at other archaeological sites around the world (Ghezzi and Ruggles, 2007), and more recently at Stonehenge (Darvill 2022). While

157

researchers in archaeoastronomy (also known as skyscape archaeology) have often tended to focus on alignments related to the
solar and lunar extremes, at the solstices and lunar standstills, the
significance of sunrise and full-moonrise crossover events at the
equinoxes is now being more widely recognised (Silva and Pimenta 2012; Silva 2016). Such work is clearly relevant to the
Yeavering model proposed here, which makes use of the same full
moon nearest the equinox (on or after ordinal day 76). However,
the aforementioned studies generally relate to prehistoric monuments constructed during the European Neolithic and Bronze
Age, with little evidence of such complex observational astronomy
among the pagan Germanic-speaking peoples of later northern
Europe. The British astronomer and archaeologist Clive Ruggles
(2011) has promoted a twofold approach to assessing proposed ancient alignments: (a) an astronomical or statistical approach that
asks scientific questions about the intentionality of any proposed
alignments, and (b) an archaeological or contextual approach that
asks social questions about the meaning of any proposed alignments. In other words, were the alignments intentional, and do
they have any wider meaning or social context?

If we imagine that Yeavering's structure E was replicated (with
the same azimuths and assumed eastern horizon) at opposite ends
of the British Isles, one near Stonehenge on Salisbury Plain and
the other near Maeshowe on the main island of Orkney (at latitudes of 51.179 and 58.997 degrees), we can demonstrate how its
actual location at Yeavering (latitude 55.567 degrees) provides evidence of intentionality. While the E-AX-BX sunrise alignment
(86 degrees), which is closest to the spring equinox, would occur
on broadly the same day at Stonehenge, Yeavering and Maeshowe,
the E-North-Side sunrise alignment (99.5 degrees), which precedes the spring equinox, would occur at least one day earlier at
Stonehenge and one day later at Maeshowe. However, it is the E-
South-Side sunrise alignment (45 degrees) that shows the greatest
differences at the two imagined locations. At latitudes south of

Yeavering, including Stonehenge, this alignment is outside the range of possible solar azimuths (see table 26), while at latitudes north of Yeavering it occurs at much earlier dates in the year, being some twenty-six days earlier at Maeshowe. Thus, it is only at Yeavering's latitude, and with its local horizon, that these sunrise azimuths yield the precise lunisolar intervals and summer solstice alignment described in this chapter. Contextual evidence, demonstrating how structure E and its alignments could express wider social and cultural meaning, is provided by Bede. Firstly, in his historical work where he describes the site as an important centre for the early pagan kings of Bernicia, and secondly in his calendrical work where his description of the pagan Anglo-Saxon calendar can be mathematically related to the physical (archaeological) evidence recorded at Yeavering. This combined evidence helps to explain the function and meaning of *Eosturmonath* the 'eastern-month' with a demonstrable connection to the equinoctial sunrise and nearest full-moonrise, and an important role in regulating the months of the Anglo-Saxon year.

SUMMARY AND CONCLUSION

Having come to the end of this somewhat circuitous journey, I can now summarise the key points made in relation to Bede's goddess *Eostre* and the origins of the Easter festival.

The first thing to be said is that the Christian Paschal festival or Feast of the Resurrection derives its liturgical Latin and Greek names (*Pascha* and Πάσχα) and its timing from the Jewish Passover, during which Jesus' crucifixion and resurrection allegedly occurred. Bede was perfectly clear that the overlap of the Christian Paschal season and the Anglo-Saxon *Eosturmonath* (Bede's month of *Eostre*) was simply a coincidence. It is therefore spurious to suggest that the Early Christians (centred around the eastern Mediterranean) would have named and timed their most important festival to coincide with that of a (yet to be recorded) north European pagan goddess. In late Roman and post-Roman Britain the festival was known by its Latin name *Pascha* and by its related insular Celtic (British and Irish) names *Pasc* and *Cásc*. Furthermore, three British bishops are known to have attended the Council of Arles in 314 AD, where the dating of the Paschal festival was discussed, and that it should be observed on the same Sunday by Christians throughout the world—these events taking place over a century before the first wave of Anglo-Saxon settlement in Britain, and four centuries before any mention of the goddess *Eostre*.

Throughout most of western Europe the names used for the Christian Feast of the Resurrection are derived from the Latin name *Pascha*, including the Italian *Pasqua*, French *Pâques*, Spanish *Pascua*, Dutch *Pasen*, and Danish *Påske*. However, in English and German the festival goes by the altogether different names of Easter and *Ostern*. The explanation provided by Bede—that the English name is derived from the goddess *Eostre*, whose month (*Eosturmonath*) and celebrations coincided with the Christian festival—has become a matter of some contention, with many academics now rejecting his testimony as mere speculation or conjecture. However, before dismissing his explanation we should bear in mind that many of Bede's contemporaries, including the older members of own family, would have remembered the days of Northumbrian heathenism (Mayr-Harting 1991, 22). Furthermore, as a devout Christian scholar and historian, Bede seems unlikely to have invented a fictitious pagan festival (and goddess) in order to account for the name of a Christian one (Green 2000, 353).

Evidence in support of Bede may also be gleaned from the Northumbrian personal name *Easterwine*, with at least four known occurrences of the name and two possible interpretations: 'Eastern-friend' or 'Eostre's-follower'. If it meant the former, then we might logically expect to find other Old English names using the remaining cardinal points (north, south or west) as their prototheme and *wine* as their deuterotheme, but we don't. If it meant the latter, then we might logically expect to find other Old English names using mythological or theophoric elements as their prototheme and *wine* as their deuterotheme, which we do— including *Ælfwine*, *Freawine*, *Ingwine* and *Oswine*. Recent work by Leonard Neidorf (2021) has drawn attention to these and other names, and likens the name *Freawine* found in the royal genealogies of Wessex (*Anglo-Saxon Chronicle*, 552 AD) to the term *Freys vinr* (Freyr's follower) found in the *Poetic Edda* (*Sigurðarkviða in skamma*, stanza 24), and to the group name *Ingwine* (Ing's followers) found in *Beowulf* (lines 1044 and 1319). These examples tend to support the 'Eostre's follower' interpretation of *Easterwine*, and demonstrate that a theophoric interpretation cannot be ruled out.

The Old High German festival name *Ostarun* and Frankish month name *Ostarmanoth* have long been said to derive from a parallel Germanic name for the goddess *Eostre*, reconstructed as *Ostara*. While Jacob Grimm (1835, 182) is often credited with this idea, its development can be traced back through various earlier sources to works by Philipp Clüver (1616, 237) and Sebastian Münster (1550, 45). While modern German researchers have offered alternative routes by which the name *Ostarun* could have arisen in Old High German, they have not adequately explained how the related festival name *Eastron* also arose in Old English. Nevertheless, there may be a more direct route by which the festival and month names could have entered the German language, and one that explains why related names also existed in Anglo-Saxon England. Much of Germany was converted to (and tutored in) Christianity by clerics from England, most notably by St Boniface, but also by his successor Bishop Lull of Mainz, and later by Alcuin the teacher and librarian at Charlemagne's court in Aachen. These individuals, and their fellow English missionaries, would have spoken a related, and often very similar, language to those they were teaching and seeking and convert; and thus could have been using the Old English festival and month names during the course of their work. We know that Lull had requested and received copies of Bede's works from the monastery at Jarrow; that very early fragments of Bede's *De Temporum Ratione* have been found in northern German and at Darmstadt near Mainz; and that it was Alcuin's pupil Einhard who wrote the *Vita Karoli Magni* with its reference to *Ostarmanoth*. So, did the eighth-century German converts and Frankish scholars simply adopt the Old English names *Eastron* and *Eastermonath* into their native language, which then appeared in Old High German orthography as *Ostarun* and *Ostarmanoth*? I favour this explanation because it is consistent with the available evidence and provides a simple explanation for the close parallel between the Old English and Old High German festival and month names. However, it does not deny Bede's claim that the goddess *Eostre* was worshipped in early Anglo-Saxon England or preclude the existence of an earlier Proto-Germanic goddess cult.

Nevertheless, by the mid to late nineteenth century the goddesses *Eostre* and *Ostara* were widely seen to be reflections of the same pan-Germanic goddess of the dawn and spring. With the development of comparative linguistics and comparative mythology, she was subsequently said to be the Germanic reflex of a more ancient Proto-Indo-European dawn goddess, as evidenced by examples found in the other Indo-European languages: Sanskrit *Ushas*, Farsi *Ushah*, Greek *Eos*, Latin *Auroa* and Lithunaian (Samogitian) *Ausca*. With the emergence of the Romantic Movement and the rise of ethnic or Romantic Nationalism across Europe, shared language was the determining feature of the various new nationalist movements, which included Celtic, Germanic, Baltic and Slavic nationalism. The search for an 'authentic' national folklore and mythology also played a central role in the development of these movements, which often characterised themselves as great 'revivals' or 'awakenings' of collective national and political consciousness. While their tendency to misrepresent, exaggerate or falsify linguistic, folkloric and mythological evidence is well documented, the evidence for a Proto-Indo-European dawn goddess cannot be completely discounted. If we acknowledge that comparative linguistics (of related deity names), when combined with comparative mythology (of their traits and characteristics), can indicate descent from a shared ancestral mythology, then it is not unreasonable to look for other examples of these deities within the cultures of related-language speakers—such as *Eostre*.

Two Easter symbols that are most often said to be associated with the goddesses *Eostre* or *Ostara* are the Easter egg (*Ostereier*) and Easter rabbit or hare (*Osterhase*). However, there is no real evidence to support these claims. The Christian symbolism associated with the Easter egg, or more correctly the Paschal egg, is first known to have arisen among the Christian communities of the Eastern church; and can be explained as a Christian metaphor for the resurrection of Jesus, which was given on Easter Sunday when eggs could finally be eaten after the long Lenten fast. Following the Anglo-Saxons' conversion to Christianity there is no evidence of the Paschal egg tradition in early medieval England. The first record of the *Osterhase* appears over a thousand years later in south-west Germany, and is largely unknown in England until the late nineteenth century. It is therefore doubtful that Christians appropriated either tradition from any early Anglo-Saxon or ancient Germanic pagan practices. Nevertheless, these two Easter symbols are often quoted in the annual 'Ostara versus Easter' appropriation claims made by members of the world's largest neopagan religion Wicca, who celebrate the spring equinox as the 'Sabbat of Ostara', one of the eight festivals in their 'Wheel of the Year'. While many of its elements are indeed ancient, the year they now follow is a composite creation of relatively recent origin, having first been devised by the religion's founder Gerald Gardner in 1954. At that point in time the Wiccan calendar did not include 'Sabbat of Ostara', which was added in 1974 by the California based Wiccan poet and writer Aidan Kelly, along with the two other festival names (Kelly 2017). Various America publications then made the new festivals names popular in Britain, where they have become permanent features of the Wiccan calendar.

The discovery of the Roman altar stones at Morken-Harrf near Cologne in 1958, with their dedications to the *Matronae Austriahenae*, provided the first evidence of any female deities with a Germanic name that is potentially cognate with Bede's goddess *Eostre*. However, we must avoid jumping to conclusions.

While these deity names may indeed be linguistically related (through a common Proto-Germanic word meaning 'east'), the two goddess cults do not necessarily share a common origin and could have arisen independently. With regard to Philip Shaw's (2011) interpretation of the *Austriahenae* epithet, there is no clear evidence that these matrons were named after a local 'eastern' group or area; and their name could just as easily relate to a more distant 'eastern' tribal homeland, which is where the Roman historians (Strabo and Tacitus) tell us the local Ubian people (the dedicants) originated. In addition to which, we have no evidence that the *Matronae Austriahenae* existed as either a native pre-Roman cult, or that such deities were worshipped by the Germanic tribes living outside the Roman Empire (to the east of the Rhine). While the first element of the *Austria-henae* epithet may be Germanic in origin, the suffix is now thought to be the result of a Celtic (Gaulish) word-formation process and deity-naming practice, which the *Ubii* could have adopted sometime after 39 BC when they were relocated from the east bank to the west bank of the river Rhine. As a consequence it throws into doubt whether *Eostre* and the *Austriahenae* (in particular) can be viewed as evidence of parallel deity-naming practices in the early Germanic languages.

I am not persuaded by Philip Shaw's (20111) argument that *Eostre* was named after a relatively small 'eastern' sub-kingdom and its people in Kent. The comparison he makes with the *Matronae Austriahenae*, and with the other localised matron cults of the Lower Rhine region, relies on the assumption that *Eostre* was similarly a localised cult. However, there is no real evidence to support this assumption. Although the reconstructed element *ēastor* appears to have been used in some Anglo-Saxon personal names and one month name, the evidence for its use in a small number of English place names (including Eastry in Kent) is more ambiguous. Furthermore, it seems somewhat implausible to suggest that the name of a very localised pagan deity, would be accepted by the church as the vernacular name for its most important festival, and then promoted throughout the rest of the country. However, my main criticism of this theory is that Shaw fails to explain why his 'local group-specific goddess' would have been so revered at this specific time of the year. Shaw finds no grounds to doubt Bede's claim that the goddess *Eostre* gave her name to *Eosturmonath*, and rejects the suggestion that Bede would have fabricated this explanation given his renown as a 'careful researcher' (Shaw 2012). Nevertheless, Shaw appears to ignore the single and most important piece of evidence that Bede provides about the cult of *Eostre*, namely the timing of her month and celebrations.

Bede's account of the goddesses *Rheda* and *Eostre* is now widely questioned by many archaeologists, historians and linguists, who suggest that these deity names were back-formations derived retrospectively from *Rhedmonath* and *Eosturmonath* as conjectural etymologies for the month names. Nevertheless, such criticism does not call into question the existence of these Old English month names, or that in England the Christian festival of *Pascha* simply took its vernacular name from month in which it most often occurred (Shaw 2011, 69). So, regardless of whether Bede's account of these goddesses is accepted or rejected, we can hopefully agree that *Eosturmonath* combines two elements: one related to 'east' or 'eastern' and the other meaning 'month'. If so, then the equinoctial sunrise and nearest full-moonrise, by appearing in their more easterly positions on the horizon during this month, offer a more logical explanation for timing and etymology of *Eosturmonath*. Thus, it is difficult to see how Shaw's (2011) 'local goddess' theory can be said to have 'done away' with arguments linking the goddess *Eostre*—who Bede tells us was worshipped during that month—with the spring or the dawn.

In his historical work Bede describes Yeavering (*Adgefrin*) in Northumberland's Cheviot Hills as an important centre for the

167

early pagan kings of Bernicia. When the site was excavated by Brian Hope-Taylor in 1953-1962 he identified a unique wedge shape building (structure E), which he interpreted as a theatre or grandstand, but with no real archaeological parallels. The three principal sunrise alignments associated with this enigmatic structure, having been correctly identified (with azimuths of 45, 86 and 99.5 degrees), provide what may be the first evidence in support of Bede's pagan Anglo-Saxon calendar. It is only at Yeavering's latitude, with its local eastern horizon (0.5 degrees), that these sunrise alignments yield the precise solstitial alignment and lunisolar intervals capable of regulating the nineteen-year Metonic cycle, with is twelve common and seven embolismic (Bede's *Thrilithi*) lunar years. But perhaps most importantly, this is achieved by monitoring the occurrence of the full moon nearest the vernal (spring) equinox—between *Rhedmonath* and *Eosturmonth*. The natural phenomena associated with the spring equinox—the longer daylight hours and the resurgence of plant and animal life—have in many cultures and religions come to symbolise the triumph of light over darkness and life over death. This is particularly true of the symbolism surrounding Easter and the Christian interpretation of Jesus' crucifixion and resurrection. It is therefore not unreasonable to suggest that these same natural phenomena were likewise significant to the pagan Anglo-Saxons, and that *Eosturmonath* was the month in which they became apparent; with its celebrations so culturally embedded that the Christian missionaries made the conscious decision to adopt the Old English festival name to attract more converts to the new faith. If so, then Bede's goddess *Eostre*—as a personification of these natural phenomena and time of year—should still be given serious consideration and continues to provide an intriguing yet credible explanation.

ABOUT THE AUTHOR

RICHARD SERMON is a graduate of the Dorset Institute of Higher Education (now Bournemouth University) and the University of Southampton, with almost forty years' professional engagement in British field archaeology and heritage protection. His formal career began at the Museum of London where as a senior archaeologist he supervised excavations in the historic City of London and in 1990 correctly identified the Gresham Street medieval *mikveh* (Jewish ritual bath). He went on to hold senior positions as deputy director of the Scottish Urban Archaeological Trust, and following a move into local government, as city archaeologist for Gloucester and finally as county archaeologist for Bath and North East Somerset. He has related interests in musicology, linguistics, and folklore, having written on various subjects ranging from medieval bone flutes and the origins of the pipe and tabor, to the philology of wassailing and the use of folkloric motifs in the 1973 cult horror film *The Wicker Man* (Luath Press 2006). His work has been published in *Bristol & Avon Archaeology*, *Current Archaeology*, *Decies*, *Folklore*, *Glevensis*, *Jewish Historical Studies*, *Northern History*, *Oxoniensia*, *Time & Mind*, and the *Proceedings of the Society of Antiquaries of Scotland*, along with other periodicals and journals. In this volume he returns to the subject of early calendars and festivals in Britain and Ireland, pulling together much of his earlier work and introducing a wide range of new or previously under-researched material.

REFERENCES

Applebaum, Shimon. 1951. "Were there Jews in Roman Britain?" *Transaction of the Jewish Historical Society of England* 17, 189–205.

Athanassakis, Apostolos, and Benjamin Wolkow, trans. 2013. *The Orphic Hymns*. Baltimore: Johns Hopkins University Press.

Attenborough, Frederick Levi, ed. and trans. 1922. *The Laws of the Earliest English Kings*. London: Cambridge University Press.

Barnwell, Paul. 2005. "Anglian Yeavering: A Continental Perspective." In *Yeavering: People, Power and Place*, edited by Paul Frodsham and Colm O'Brien, 174–184. Stroud: The History Press.

Bielfeldt, Hans Holm. 1977. "Die ältesten nicht mehr gemein-slawischen Entlehnungen des Nordwestslawischen aus dem Deutschen." *Zeitschrift für Slawistik* 22: 431–454.

Biller, Frank. 2001. "Eine fast vergessene Matronenweihung aus Bad Münstereifel." *Archäologie im Rheinland* (2001): 69–72.

Biller, Frank. 2010. *Kultische Zentren und Matronenverehrung in der Südlichen Germania Inferior*. Rahden: Leidorf.

Botfield, Beriah. ed. 1841. *Manners and Household Expenses of England in the Thirteenth and Fifteenth Centuries*. London: William Nicol, Shakespeare Press.

Bromwich, Rachel, ed. 1978. *Trioedd Ynys Prydein: The Welsh Triads*. Cardiff: University of Wales Press.

Bronchorst, Johann, ed. 1537. *Bedae, Opuscula Complura de Temporum Ratione*. Cologne: Johann Prael and Peter Quentel.

171

Brooks, Nicholas. 1989. "The Creation and Early Structure of the Kingdom of Kent." In *The Origins of Anglo-Saxon Kingdoms*, edited by Steven Bassett, 55–74. London: Leicester University Press.

Brooks, Nicholas, and Susan Kelly, eds. 2013. *Charters of Christ Church, Canterbury, Part 1: Anglo-Saxon Charters*. Oxford: Oxford University Press and The British Academy.

Bund der Deutschen in Böhmen, after 1894. *Ostermond: Ostara*, monats karte (postcard) no. 4. Prague: printer unknown. https://www.akpool.de/ansichtskarten/26027005

Camden, William. 1586. *Britannia* (first edition in Latin). London: Ralph Newbery.

Camden, William. 1610. *Britannia* (translated by Philemon Holland). London: George Bishop and John Norton.

Carroll, Maureen. 2006. *Spirits of the Dead: Roman Funerary Commemoration in Western Europe*. Oxford: Oxford University Press.

Clüver, Philipp. 1616. *Germaniae Antiquae*, Book 1. Leiden: Louis Elzevir.

Colgrave, Bertram, ed. 1927. *The Life of Bishop Wilfrid by Eddius Stephanus*. Cambridge: Cambridge University Press.

Collingwood, Robin George, and Richard Pearson Wright. 1965. *Roman Inscriptions of Britain*, Vol. 1. Oxford: Clarendon Press.

Colomies, Paul. 1688. *Observationes Sacrae*. London: James Adamson.

Colomies, Paul. 1709. *Opera, Theologici, Critici et Historici Argumenti*, edited by Johann Albert Fabricius. Hamburg: Christian Liebezeit.

Cook, Albert. 1894. *A Glossary of the Old Northumbrian Gospels* (Lindisfarne Gospels or Durham Book). Halle: Max Niemeyer.

Corbier, Mireille, ed. 2001. *L'Année Epigraphique*. Paris: Université de Paris.

Crawford, Samuel, ed. 1929. *Byrhtferth's Manual*. London: Early English Text Society.

Cunliffe, Barry. 1997. *The Ancient Celts*. Oxford: Oxford University

Press.

Cusack, Carole. 2007. "The Goddess Eostre: Bede's Text and Contemporary Pagan Tradition(s)." *The Pomegranate* 9 (1): 22–40.

Darmesteter, James, trans. 1898. "Khorda Avesta" in *Sacred Books of the East*, Vol. 3. New York: Christian Literature Company (unauthorised American edition).

Dahn, Felix and Therese. 1885. *Walhall: Germanische Götter- und Heldensagen*. Kreuznach: Robert Voigtländer.

Darvill, Timothy. 2022. "Keeping time at Stonehenge." *Antiquity* 96 (386): 319–335.

Davies, Gareth Huw. 1993. "Will the Real Easter Bunny Stand Up?" *Radio Times* (April 10–16): 20–21.

De Bernardo Stempel, Patrizia. 2019. "Matronen- und andere Götter(bei)namen auf *-genae/-es* bzw. *-chenae, -henae* und *-enae*." *Beiträge zur Namenforschung* 54 (2): 121–52.

De Bernardo Stempel, Patrizia. 2021. *Muttergöttinnen und ihre Votivformulare: Eine sprach-historische Studie*. Heidelberg: Universitätsverlag Carl Winter.

De Bernardo Stempel, Patrizia. 2022. *Die sprachliche Analyse der niedergermanischen Votiv-formulare und Dedikantennamen*. Wien: Österreichische Akademie der Wissenschaften.

De Selincourt, Aubrey, trans. 1954. *Herodotus, The Histories*. London: Penguin.

Debrabandere, Frans. 1993. *Woordenboek van de Familienamen in België en Noord-Frankrijk*. Brussels: Gemeentekrediet.

Derks, Ton. 1998. *Gods, Temples, and Ritual Practices: The Transformation of Religious Ideas and Values in Roman Gaul*. Amsterdam: Amsterdam University Press.

Detoma, Edoardo. 2018. "An Easter Date Calendar in Ravenna." *Memorie* (Accademia delle Scienze di Torino) 42 (1): 3–74.

Deuerlein, Ernst. 1959. "Hitlers Eintritt in die Politik und die Reichswehr." *Aus Politik und Zeitgeschichte* 28 (July 8): 241–263.

Dolgopolsky, Aharon. 2008. *Nostratic Dictionary*. Cambridge: McDonald Institute for Archaeological Research (University of Cambridge).

Dutton, Paul Edward, trans. 1998. *Charlemagne's Courtier: The Complete Einhard*. Peterborough, Ontario: Broadview Press.

Edwards, Cyril. 2002. "The Strange Case of the Old High German Lullaby." In *The Beginnings of German Literature: Comparative and Interdisciplinary Approaches to Old High German*, by Cyril Edwards, 142–165. Rochester: Camden House.

Ekwall, Eilert. 1960. *The Concise Oxford Dictionary of English Place Names*, fourth edition. Oxford: Oxford University Press.

Fairclough, Henry Rushton, trans. 1916. *Virgil, Aeneid*. Vol. 1. Loeb Classical Library 63. Cambridge, MA: Harvard University Press.

Fischart, Johann. 1598. *Aller Praktik Grossmutter*, reprint of expanded 1574 edition. Strasbourg: Bernhard Jobin.

Flügel, Ewald. 1903. "References to the English Language in the German Literature of the First Half of the Sixteenth Century." *Modern Philology* 1 (1): 19–30.

Frazer, James. 1922. *The Golden Bough: A Study in Magic and Religion*. London: Wordsworth Reference.

Gardner, Gerald. 1954. *Witchcraft Today*. London: Rider.

Geldner, Karl, ed. 1896. *Avesta, the Sacred Books of the Parsis*, 3 parts. Stuttgart: Wilhelm Kohlhammer.

Ghezzi, Ivan, and Clive Ruggles. 2007. "Chankillo: A 2300-Year-Old Solar Observatory in Coastal Peru." *Science* 315 (March 2): 1239–1243.

Gollancz, Israel, ed. 1895. *The Exeter Book: An Anthology of Anglo-Saxon Poetry, Part 1*. London: The Early English Text Society.

Goodrick-Clarke, Nicholas. 2004. *The Occult Roots of Nazism*. London: Tauris Parke Paperbacks.

Gorman, Michael. 1996. "The glosses on Bede's *De Temporum Ratione* attributed to Byrhtferth of Ramsey." *Anglo-Saxon England* 25: 209–232.

Graff, Eberhard Gottlieb, ed. 1831. *Otfrid's Krist*. Königsberg: Gebrüder Bornträger.

Grafton, Anthony, and Urs Leu. 2013. "Chronologia est unica historiae lux: how Glarean studied and taught the chronology of the ancient world." In *Heinrich Glarean's Books: in The Intellectual*

World of a Sixteenth-Century Musical Humanist, edited by Iain Fenlon and Inga Groote, 248–279. Cambridge: Cambridge University Press.

Green, Dennis Howard. 2000. *Language and History in the Early Germanic World*. Cambridge: Cambridge University Press.

Green, Miranda. 1988. *The Gods of Roman Britain*. Princes Risborough: Shire Books.

Gretzinger, Joscha, Duncan Sayer, Pierre Justeau, et al. 2022. "The Anglo-Saxon migration and the formation of the early English gene pool." *Nature* 610: 112–119.

Griffith, Ralph, trans. 1896. *The Hymns of the Rigveda*, second edition. 2 vols. Benares: Lazarus and Company.

Grimm, Jacob. 1835. *Deutsche Mythologie*. Göttingen: Dieterichschen Buchhandlung.

Grimm, Jacob. 1848. *Geschichte der deutschen Sprache*, Vol. 1. Leipzig: Weidmannschen Buchhandlung.

Grimm, Johann Andreas. 1725. *Bibliotheca Historico-Philologico-Theologica Classis*, Vol. 8, Fascicule 1. Bremen: Hermann Brauer.

Gunnell, Terry. 2021. "The Myths of the Vanir and Seasonal Change in the North." In *Res, Artes et Religio: Essays in Honour of Rudolf Simek*, edited by Sabine Walther, Regina Jucknies, Judith Meurer-Bongardt, Jens Schnall, 235–251. Leeds: Kismet Press.

Helm, Karl. 1950. "Erfundene Götter?" in *Studien zur deutschen Philologie des Mittelalters*, edited by Richard Kienast, 1–11. Heidelberg: Universitätsverlag Carl Winter.

Henel, Heinrich, ed. 1942. *Aelfric's De Temporibus Anni*. London: Early English Text Society.

Herwagen, Johann, ed. 1563. *Opera Bedae Venerabilis*, Vol. 2. Basle: Johann Herwagen.

Herzfeld, George, ed. 1900. *An Old English Martyrology*. London: Early English Text Society.

Hessmann, Pierre. 2000. "Asteronhus im Freckenhorster Heberegister." In *Speculum Saxonum, Amsterdamer Beiträge zur älteren Germanistik* 52: 97–104.

Hines, John. 2022. "The migration question: re-grounding Anglo-

Saxon archaeology." *Current Archaeology* (392): 20–24.

Hocker, Nikolaus. 1853. *Deutscher Volksglaube in Sang und Sage.* Göttingen: Dieterich.

Holtzmann, Adolf. 1874. *Deutsche Mythologie.* Leipzig: Benedictus Gotthelf Teubner.

Hope-Taylor, Brian. 1977. *Yeavering: an Anglo-British Centre of Early Northumbria.* Department of the Environment Archaeological Reports 7. London: HMSO.

Hutton, Ronald. 1996. *The Stations of the Sun.* Oxford: Oxford University Press.

Hutton, Ronald. 2001. *The Triumph of the Moon: A History of Modern Pagan Witchcraft.* Oxford: Oxford University Press.

Hutton, Ronald. 2008. "Modern Pagan Festivals: A Study in the Nature of Tradition." *Folklore* 119 (3): 251–27.

Hutton, Ronald. 2009. *Blood and Mistletoe: The History of Druids in Britain.* New Haven: Yale University Press.

Hyde, Thomas. 1694. *De Ludis Orientalibus.* Oxford: Sheldonian Theatre.

Ivarsen, Ingrid. 2022. "King Ine (688–726) and the Writing of English Law in Latin." *English Historical Review* 137 (584): 1–46.

Jackson, John, trans. 1937. *Tacitus. Annals: Books 4–6, 11–12.* Loeb Classical Library 312. Cambridge, MA: Harvard University Press.

James, Simon. 1999. *The Atlantic Celts: Ancient People or Modern Invention?* London: British Museum Press.

Jones, Charles, ed. 1977. Bede, *De Temporum Ratione.* Corpus Christianorum, Series Latina 123B. Turnhout: Brepols.

Jones, Horace Leonard, trans. 1923. *Strabo, Geography, Books 3–5.* Loeb Classical Library 50. Cambridge, MA: Harvard University Press.

Kelly, Aidan. 2017. "About Naming Ostara, Litha, and Mabon" *Patheos* (blog), May 2. https://www.patheos.com/blogs/aidankelly/2017/05/naming-ostara-litha-mabon/

King, John Edward, trans. 1930. *Bede, Historical Works.* 2 vols. Loeb Classical Library 246 and 248. Cambridge, MA: Harvard University

Press.

Kinsella, Thomas, trans. 1970. *The Táin: From the Irish epic Táin Bó Cuailnge*. Oxford: Oxford University Press.

Knobloch, Johann. 1959. "Der Ursprung von Neuhochdeutsch Ostern, Englisch Easter." *Die Sprache* 5: 27–45.

Knox, John. 1644. *The Historie of the Reformation of the Church of Scotland*, in 5 books. London: John Raworth.

Kolbe, Hans-Georg. 1960. "Die neuen Matroneninschriften von Morken-Harff." *Bonner Jahrbücher* 160: 50–124.

König, Werner. 1979. *Atlas zur deutschen Sprache*, third edition. München: Deutscher Taschenbuch Verlag.

Krogmann, Willy. 1937. "Osorb. jutry Ostern." *Zeitschrift für Slavische Philologie* 14 (3/4): 301–302.

Labarge, Margaret Wade. 1965. *A Baronial Household of the Thirteenth Century*. London: Eyre & Spottiswoode.

Langewiesche, Friedrich. 1931. "Was ist's mit Teudts Germanischen Heiligtümern?" *Westfalen: Hefte für Geschichte, Kunst und Volkskunde* 16: 226–230.

Łasicki, Jan. 1615. *De diis Samagitarum caeterorumque Sarmatarum et falsorum Christianorum*. Basel: Conrad Waldkirch.

Lhuyd, Edward. 1707. *Archæologia Britannica*, Vol. 1. Oxford: Sheldonian Theatre.

Lloyd, James. 2013. "The Origin of the Lathes of East Kent." *Archaeologia Cantiana* 133: 83–113.

Lunt, Horace. 2001. *Old Church Slavonic Grammar*, seventh revised edition. Berlin and New York: Mouton de Gruyter.

Lysons, Samuel, ed. and John Brand, trans. 1806. "Rotulus Fmiliae in the Eighteenth Year of the Reign of King Edward I." *Archaeologia* 15: 350–62.

Mallory, James, and Douglas Adams. 2006. *The Oxford Introduction to Proto-Indo-European and the Proto-Indo-European World*. Oxford: Oxford University Press.

Mattingly, Harold, trans. 1970. *Tacitus, The Agricola and The Germania*. London: Penguin Books.

Mayr-Harting, Henry. 1991. *The Coming of Christianity to Anglo-Saxon*

England, third edition. Bath: Batsford.

Merlin, Alfred, ed. 1962. *L'Année Epigraphique*. Paris: Université de Paris.

Mitra, Rajendralala. 1878. *Buddha Gaya, the hermitage of Sakya Muni*. Governmentt of Bengal. Calcutta: Bengal Secretariat Press.

Mommsen Theodor, ed. 1898. "Nennius: Historia Brittonum." In *Monumenta Germaniae Historica* 13. Chronica Minora 3, 111–222. Berlin: Weidmann.

Montanus (Vincenz Jacob von Zuccalmaglio). 1858. *Die Deutschen Volksfeste, Volksbräuche und Deutscher Volksglaube in Sagen, Märlein und Volksliedern*. Iserlohn: Bädeter.

Morris, John. 1977. *Age of Arthur: A History of the British Isles from 350 to 650*. Chichester: Phillimore.

Müller, Friedrich Max. 1909 [1856]. *Comparative Mythology: an Essay*. London: George Routledge and Sons.

Munier, Charles, ed. 1963. "Concilia Galliae a. 314–a. 506." *Corpus Christianorum Series Latina* 148. Turnhout: Brepols.

Münster, Sebastian. 1550. *Cosmographia*, Latin edition. Basel: Heinrich Petri.

Murray, Augustus Taber, trans. 1919. *Homer, The Odyssey*. 2 vols. Loeb Classical Library 104 and 105. Cambridge, MA: Harvard University Press.

Murray, Augustus Taber, trans. 1925. *Homer, The Illiad*. Vol. 2. Loeb Classical Library 171. Cambridge, MA: Harvard University Press.

Mushard, Luneberg. 1702. *De Ostera Saxonum*. Bremen: Brauer.

Nash-Williams, Victor Erle, 1950. *The Early Christian Monuments of Wales*. Cardiff: University of Wales Press.

Neidorf, Leonard. 2021. "The Etymology of Freawaru's Name." *Notes and Queries* 68 (4): 379–383.

Neidorf, Leonard. 2022. "Woden and The English Landscape: The Naming of Wansdyke Reconsidered." *Folklore* 133 (3): 378–398.

Nesselhauf, Heerbert, and Hans Lieb. 1959. "Dritter Nachtrag zu CIL XIII: Inschriften aus den Germanischen Provinzen und dem Treverergebiet." *Bericht der Römisch-Germanischen Kommission* 40 (1960): 120–228.

Neumann, Günter. 2008. "Die germanischen Matronen-Beinamen" reprinted in *Günter Neumann: Namenstudien zum Altgermanischen*, edited by Heinrich Hettrich and Astrid van Nahl, 253–89. Berlin: Walter de Gruyter. First published in *Beihefte der Bonner Jahrbücher* 44 (1987): 103–32.

Newall, Venetia. 1971. *An Egg at Easter: A Folklore Study*. London: Routledge & Kegan Paul.

Nicholls, Steve, producer. 1993. *Wildlife on One* (Easter Special). "The Shadow of the Hare." Filmed and directed by Ian McCarthy. Aired April 12. British Broadcasting Corporation.

North, Richard. 2012. "Eostre the goddess and the free-standing posts of Yeavering." Paper presented at *Starcræft*, UCL Early Medieval Interdisciplinary Conference, June 30. http://www.academia.edu/25730626/Eostre_the_goddess_and_t he_free-standing_posts_of_Yeavering.

Oswald, Alastair and Trevor Pearson. 2005. "Yeavering Bell Hillfort." In *Yeavering: People, Power and Place*, edited by Paul Frodsham and Colm O'Brien, 98–126. Stroud: The History Press.

Parker, Eleanor. 2022. *Winters in the World: A Journey Through the Anglo-Saxon Year*. London: Reaktion Books.

Patterson, Nick, Michael Isakov, Thomas Booth, et al. 2022. "Large-scale migration into Britain during the Middle to Late Bronze Age." *Nature* 601: 588–594.

Peterson, William, trans. 1914. *Tacitus, Dialogus, Agricola, Germania*. Loeb Classical Library 35. Cambridge, MA: Harvard University Press.

Petts, David. 2016. "Christianity in Roman Britain." In *The Oxford Handbook of Roman Britain*, edited by Martin Millett, Louise Revell, and Alison Moore, 660–681. Oxford: Oxford University Press.

Piper, Paul. 1884. *Libri Confraternitatum Sancti Galli Augiensis Fabariensis*. Berlin: Weidmann.

Pope Paul V, ed. 1617. *Rituale Romanum*. Rome: Typographia Camerae Apostolicae.

Prior, Maddy. 1993. "The Fabled Hare." Track 9 on *Year*. Park

Records, Compact Disk.

Pronk-Tiethoff, Saskia. 2013. *Germanic Loanwords in Proto-Slavic.* Amsterdam and New York: Rodolpi.

Ralston, Ian, and Roger Miket. 2024. "Brian Hope-Taylor (1923–2001) and Northumbria: a centenary re-assessment of excavations and interpretations at Yeavering and Doon Hill, Dunbar." *Society of Antiquaries of London* (online lecture) March 5. https://www.youtube.com/watch?v=WC8E69MFyhQ

Rathlef, Ernst Ludwig. 1766. "Eine Rede von der Verehrung der Sächsischen Göttin Eostra auf dem Osterberge vor Nienburg." *Geschichte der Grafschaften Hoya und Diepholz*, Vol. 3. Nienburg: self-published.

Renfrew, Colin. 1987. *Archaeology and Language: The Puzzle of Indo-European Origins.* London: Jonathan Cape.

Rollason, David, and Lynda Rollason, eds. 2007. *Durham Liber Vitae: The Complete Edition.* London: British Library.

Roud, Steve. 2008, *The English Year.* London: Penguin Books.

Ruggles, Clive. 2011. "Archaeoastronomy in Europe." paper presented at *Ancient Conceptions of the Heavens: Archaeoastronomy in Europe*, University of Oxford, Department for Continuing Education, October 1.

Runde, Justus Friedrich. 1781. "Vergleichung der Römischen in unsern Kalendern annochgebräuchlichen Monatsnamen, mit denen, welche Karl der Grosse einzuführen suchte." *Deutsches Museum* 1 (January to June 1781): 7–17.

Salway, Peter. 1981. *Roman Britain* (Oxford History of England), Oxford: Clarendon Press.

Sanders, William Basevi, ed. 1878, 1881 and 1884. *Facsimiles of Anglo-Saxon Manuscripts.* 3 vols. Southampton: Ordnance Survey.

Sawyer, Peter. 1968. *Anglo-Saxon Charters: An Annotated List and Bibliography.* London: Royal Historical Society.

Schaz, Georg. 1803. *Charaktere der Vornehmsten Dichter aller Nationen*, Vol. 7. Leipzig: Dykische Buchhandlung.

Scheffauer, Ethel Talbot. 1934. *Eastertide in Germany.* Berlin: Terramare Office.

Schild, Johannes. 1649. *De Caucis, Nobilissimo Veteris Germaniae Populo*, Book 2. Leiden: Francis Hack.

Searle, William George. 1897. *Onomasticon Anglo-Saxonicum*. Cambridge: Cambridge University Press.

Semple, Sarah. 2024. "People and Place in the Kingdom of Northumbria: New project and fieldwork perspectives [Yeavering]." *Society of Antiquaries of London* (online lecture) February 8. https://www.youtube.com/watch?v=0A7eRTvajtA

Sermon, Richard. 2000. "Britons and Saxons in Gloucestershire: Migration or Assimilation." *Glevensis* 33: 7–8.

Sermon, Richard. 2002. "The Celtic Calendar and the Anglo-Saxon Year." *Third Stone* 43: 32–39.

Sermon, Richard. 2003. "Whence the Hwicce? Archaeology and Language." In *Land of the Dobunni*, edited by Martin Ecclestone, Neil Holbrook and Andrew Smith, 77–81. Committee for Archaeology in Gloucestershire and Council for British Archaeology (South West).

Sermon, Richard. 2008. "From Easter to Ostara: The Reinvention of a Pagan Goddess?" *Time and Mind* 1 (3): 331–343.

Sermon, Richard. 2022. "Eostre and the *Matronae Austriahenae*." *Folklore* 133 (2): 139–157.

Sharma, Simon. 1995. *Landscape and Memory*. London: Harper Collins.

Shaw, Philip Andrew. 2002. "Uses of Wodan: The Development of His Cult and of Medieval Literary Responses to It." PhD diss. University of Leeds. http://etheses.whiterose.ac.uk/393/

Shaw, Philip Andrew. 2007. "The Origins of the Theophoric Week in the Germanic Languages." *Early Medieval Europe* 15: 386–401.

Shaw, Philip Andrew. 2011. *Pagan Goddesses in the Early Germanic World: Eostre, Hreda and the Cult of Matrons*. Studies in Early Medieval History. London: Bristol Classical Press.

Shaw, Philip Andrew. 2012. "Easter's Culture Club Harks Back to Pagan Times." *Leicester Mercury* (April 5): 15. https://www.leicestermercury.co.uk/easter-s-culture-club-harks-pagan-times/story-15723627-detail/story.html

Shore, John, ed. 1807. *The Works of Sir William Jones*. 8 vols. London: John Stockdale and John Walker.

Showerman, Grant, trans. 1914. *Ovid, Heroides and Amores*. Loeb Classical Library 41. Cambridge, MA: Harvard University Press.

Sichard, Johann, ed. 1529. *Bedae, De Natura Rerum et Temporum Ratione*. Basel: Heinrich Petri.

Sievers, Eduard, ed. 1892. *Tatian: Lateinisch und altdeutsch mit ausführlichem Glossar*. Paderborn: Ferdinand Schöningh.

Silva, Fabio, and Fernando Pimenta. 2012. "Thee Crossover of the Sun and the Moon." *Journal for the History of Astronomy* 43 (2): 191–208.

Silva, Fabio. 2016. "Equinoctial Full Moon Models and Non-Gaussianity: Portuguese Dolmens as a Test Case." In *Astronomy and Power: How Worlds are Structured*, Proceedings of the SEAC 2010 Conference, edited by Michael Rappenglück, Barbara Rappenglück, Nicholas Campion and Fabio Silva, 51–56. BAR International Series 2794. Oxford: British Archaeological Reports.

Simpson, Jacqueline, and Steve Roud. 2000. *A Dictionary of English Folklore*. Oxford: Oxford University Press.

Speed, John. 1611. *The History of Great Britaine*. London: William Hall and John Beale.

Stallybrass, James Steven, trans. 1882 and 1883, *Jacob Grimm's Teutonic Mythology*. 2 vols. London: George Bell and Sons.

Streitberg, Wilhelm, ed. 1919. *Wulfila, Die Gotische Bibel*. Heidelberg: Universitätsverlag Carl Winter.

Tangl, Michael. 1916. *Die Briefe des heiligen Bonifatius und Lullus*. Berlin: Weidmannsche.

Teudt, Wilhelm. 1931. *Germanische Heiligtümer*, second edition. Jena: Engen Diederichs.

Thompson, Flora. 1957. *Lark Rise to Candleford*. London: Oxford University Press.

Todd, Malcolm. 1992. The Early Germans. Oxford: Blackwell.

Tolkien, J. R. R. 1955. *The Return of the King*. London: George Allen &

Unwin.

Udolph, Jürgen. 1999. *Ostern, Geschichte eines Wortes*. Heidelberg: Universitätsverlag Carl Winter.

Van der Linde, J.A. 1915. *Ostara-Wals*, (music score H.R. 212) Utrecht: H. Rahr.

Van Hamel, Anton Gerard. 1978. *Compert Con Culainn and other stories*. Medieval and Modern Irish Series, Vol. 3. Oxford: Oxford University Press.

Vesting, Otto. 1929. *Osterdechen-Gesang* (poster and postcard, printed after 1930). Lügde: printer unknown. https://www.facebook.com/OsterraederlaufLuegde

Von Franckenau, Georg Franck. 1682. *Satyrae Medicae, Continuatio XVIII: Disputatione Ordinaria Disquirens de Ovis Paschalibus von Oster-Eyern*. Heidelberg: Samuelis Ammonii.

Von List, Guido. 1896. "Ostaras Einzug." *Ostdeutsche Rundschau* (May 22): 1–3.

Vorburg, Johann Philipp. 1659. *Historia Romano-Germanica*, Vol. 9. Frankfurt: Nicolaus Kuchenbecker.

Wägner, Wilhelm. 1882. *Nordisch-germanische Götter und Helden*. Leipzig and Berlin: Otto Spamer.

Wallis, Faith, trans. 1999. *Bede, The Reckoning of Time*. Liverpool: Liverpool University Press.

Wasserbach, Ernst Casimir. 1698. *Dissertatio De Statua Illustri Harminii, Liberatoris Germaniae, vulgo Hiermensul*. Lemgo: Heinrich Wilhelm Meyer.

Weisgerber, Leo. 1962. "Der Dedikantenkreis der Matronae Austriahenae." *Bonner Jahrbücher* 162: 107–38.

Welch, Martin. 1992. *Anglo-Saxon England*, English Heritage. London: Batsford.

Winnick, Stephen. 2016. "On the Bunny Trail: In Search of the Easter Bunny." *Library of Congress, Folklife Today* (blog), March 22. https://blogs.loc.gov/folklife/2016/03/easter-bunny/

Winterbottom, Michael, ed. and trans. 1978. *Gildas: The Ruin of Britain and Other Works*. Chichester: Phillimore.

Wood, Anthony. 1691. *Athenae Oxonienses 1500-1690*. London:

Thomas Bennet.

Wood, Ian. 2005. "An Historical Context for Hope-Taylor's Yeavering." In *Yeavering: People, Power and Place*, edited by Paul Frodsham and Colm O'Brien, 185–188. Stroud: The History Press.

Zappert, Georg. 1859. *Über ein Althochdeutsches Schlummerlied*. Vienna: Hof- und Staatsdruckerei.

Online Resources

Ahmed, Monzur. 2001. "Moon Calculator." Version 6, updated September 2015. Accessed December 1, 2023.
http://www.mooncalc.moonsighting.org.uk

Osterdechenverein Lügde. 2024. "Osterräderlauf in Lügde." Accessed January 4, 2024. https://www.osterraederlauf.de/

Oxford English Dictionary. 2022. "Easter, n.1." Accessed January 10, 2023. https://www.oed.com/viewdictionaryentry/Entry/59097/

PASE. 2008. "Prosopography of Anglo-Saxon England." Accessed November 26, 2023. https://pase.ac.uk/index.html

Sadinoff, Danny. 1992. "Hebcal: Hebrew Calendar." Accessed May 28, 2023. https://www.hebcal.com/converter/

Walker, John. 1997. "Lunar Perigee and Apogee Calculator." Accessed December 1, 2023.
https://www.fourmilab.ch/earthview/pacalc.html

Walker, John. 2015. "Calendar Converter." Accessed May 28, 2023. https://www.fourmilab.ch/documents/calendar/

Made in United States
Orlando, FL
23 February 2025

58835875R00114